"One of the greatest books ever written on the subject of mysticism."
Frank Lans-*YogaItalia Academy*

"I have seen how transformative Jade's teachings can be. For years, he has been my personal guide providing me with invaluable tools for my practice, work and life while helping me to access my deeper spiritual dimensions. Jade is a powerful mystic, who has a profound gift for making spirituality accessible in our modern life today."
Bija Bennett, author of *Emotional Yoga, Breathing into Life*

"Hecate II is Brilliant and Revolutionary!'
Chandrananda-*Hinduism Today*

"Hecate II is a Masterful blend of Greco-Roman and Eastern mysticism."
Whole Life Times

"In the West, the recognition and acceptance of cannabis use as a spiritual tool is relatively obscure. However, throughout recorded history and the annals of time, as Jade Sol Luna so clearly reveals, cannabis has been used extensively by the spiritual seeker to "pierce the veil" of illusion. Cannabis, with it's highly dualistic effects, can calm our hearts and minds while stimulating us with the strength and courage required to continually seek out our real selves. In Hecate II, he takes us deeper into understanding the love, wisdom and magnificence of the Dark Mother. As any devotee of this Goddess can attest, Her path is challenging and rarely simple, as one is consistently asked to look at their shadow self. Intelligent, conscious use of cannabis can allow the seeker to experience Her and subsequentialy themselves, in greater totality."
Lisa Sawoya, Cannabis *Culture Expert*

*"Hecate II is a powerful book that could change **Mother Worship** forever."*
Devona Strassburg-*Ritual Promotions*

1

TARA INTERNATIONAL

INDIA RESEARCH PRESS / TARA PRESS INTERNATIONAL

INDIA
Corporate Office -
B-4/22,Khajuraho - 110 029, INDIA
Telephone :   91-11-2369 4610 Telefax :   91-11-2471 8637

Editorial Office -

Flat #6, TRUST OFFICE - 110003, India.
Tel: 00.91.11.2469 4610, 2469 4855
TeleFAX: 00.91.11.24618637, 417 57 113

AMERICA

JSL INC Press.
14431 Ventura Blvd suite 538
Sherman Oaks CA 91423
www.hiddenmoon.com

copyright@jslinc.org Tarainternational/jslpress

cover art by Magdaline

2

.

"Dedicated to the mystics of the world that are longing to pierce through veil of illusion to experience the "Mother of life and death" in her totality!"

Hecate II: The Awakening of Hydra

Forward *page 6*

1. The Awakening of Hydra *page 10*
Did the Mediterranean have Chakras?
The Greco-Roman Chakras

2. Hydra identified with Kundalini *page 23*
So what is Kundalini or Hydra?
Hydra, Chakras and Caelums
Hydra and the Mystic
Hydra, Kundalini, Sheshnag Plates
The Essence of Awakening Hydra
Hecate in Two Forms
The Effect of Hydra

3. The Chakras and Hecate *page 66*

4. Meditation on Death *page 95*
Meditation on Tartarus

5. Hecate, Goddess of Supreme Consciousness *page 115*
Her Darkness dissolves everything
Hecate is the time beyond time
She destroys the ego
Her force awakens Hydra
The purifying fire that burns the ego to ashes
Through her infinite grace
All Universe dissolves in you

6. The Practice *Page 123*

7. Hecate's Magical Herbs *page 126*
Deadly Nightshade
Cannabis
Black Poplar
The Oracle of Pythia and Hallucinogenics
Tantra and the Mediterranean

8. Spiritual Discipline *page 159*
The Discipline of Hecate Chthonia
Discipline of Hecate Lucifera
Discipline of Hecate Luna
The Discipline of Hecate Triceps

9. The Astronomical Body of Hecate *page 172*
Meditating on Hecate's body
Gods and Goddesses inside the Astronomical Body of Hecate
Cealums inside Hecate
Light-bearing Hecate (Goddess of Fire)

10. Hecate and Typhon *page 184*
The Ecstasy of Hecate and Typhon
Hydra, the daughter of Hecate (Echidna) and Typhon

11. The Three Deities of Hydra Awakening *page 197*

12. The Goal of the Mystic *page 201*

13. Removing the Veil of Hecate *page 204*

14. Alexander the Great and the Hindu Religion
Page 233

15. Hecate Extras *page 286*

I have been invoking, calling upon and continually surrendering to Hecate most of my life. It wasn't until I met Jade though, that I could call her by name. She was with me as a child in the dark secrets that I kept while running free through the mountains of Colorado, and it was she, who danced thru me to the beat of drums, as a wild teenager searching for a life of substance and meaning, all the while crying out in the pain of longing and desperation. Her presence was always there for me in the healing primal forces of nature. Those places where I felt most at home, most alive and most connected to my true self. In the salt of the sea, the flash of white lightning, the mysterious darkness of moon, and the vast, naked stillness of desert, she spoke to me. I heard her voice in the wind, as she ran her sharp fingers thru the core of my being, calling me down, deeper and deeper, into the mysteries of woman. She was there when I discovered the creative expression of acting, and she has been there in me as I opened up to each character, inviting them in and every time that I have played a woman who has died (which has been the majority of my roles), Hecate has guided me thru meditations on death as my body lay there lifeless on set, spirit soaring thru ethers.

Hecate demands the truth, and has always pushed me onward in my pursuit of that which gives us life. She took me to the Motherland of Africa, where I went to find my soul and then she watched my every move thru the eyes of the wild, daring me to discover my own strength and courage. In the pregnancy and birth of my son, she held me in her own womb and gave me dreams and visions of spirits transition into physical being. Then, as the sound of wolves coming from my own voice anchored my child into this dense plane, Hecate pushed me thru her own birth cannel and birthed me into the force of motherhood. She has since sat at the foot of my bed on long, lonely nights of single parenting when my son was sick with fevers and my fears had to be faced with the fierceness of lion. She has held my head thru hurt and anger of the heartache of divorce, begging me to shed the skins of my past that I may be reborn yet again and again and again.

It is she, who loves thru me with untamed passion and wicked delight and the very same she, who in the past couple years of illness, held me to her breast as I dove down into the depths of my traumatized psyche and cells, praying for transformation. She was there in the guttural moans of physical pain, the hot, sting of piercing needles and the red of my very blood that needed attention. In all of her glory, she was there as growths were cut from my throat and the unspoken words of past were released form their prison into the light of the present she is the holy water of my tears that weep for the suffering of all mothers and children. For we are all hers, her babes, her children and yet, she is also the very agony of that suffering, the raw ache of longing that calls us back to her.

Jade pointed out to me once, how when there has been a tragic accident, we, as a community say that the ones who survived, who continue to live here, had their guardian angels with them, but what of the ones who died? Do we then assume or believe that they were alone? That they, who were taken back home to the source had no angels around them? Embracing them with love? Protecting them? Something in me began to unravel with his words, unravel in a wondrous, beautiful, expansive way, a shift, a rightness, a relief washed over me, an inner knowing, never before spoken, quietly surfacing. This is how Jade works. In a culture that is so quick to label, judge and define, Jade has given me the space to play again in the magical realm of the gods. His wisdom and knowledge are matched perfectly with his heart and encompassing compassion. He has dared to walk his walk, down roads not often taken. I am deeply grateful for his guidance on my own treacherous path and by treacherous, I refer to the mystical unknowing and human insecurity of truly letting go and letting god, or in this case, goddess! - Sheryl Lee

Wikipedia: Sheryl Lee came to international attention for her performances as Laura Palmer and Maddy Ferguson on the 1990 cult TV series Twin Peaks and in the 1992 film Twin Peaks: Fire Walk with Me. She is also known for portraying photographer Astrid Kirchherr in Backbeat and for her role in Vampires, as well as for her television series roles in LA Doctors, Kingpin, One Tree Hill and Dirty Sexy Money

Hecate is the Queen of the Night and all mysteries are contained inside her. She is "Trivia" the great mystery of man.

Hecate's association and connection with other gods and goddesses are numerous: in many aspects, she signifies "the other side" – the dark, mysterious and fearsome concept, which is referred to as chthonic. Hecate is yet quite independent in her characteristics as a powerful goddess who is feared and at the same time celebrated for her power and whose existence is differentiated from Olympian deities and shunned from patriarchal system. Although the goddess is more so known to be a form of the primordial "Great Goddess" the "Holy Ghost", which survived as Hecate-Artemis, Hecate also functions as a mediator between theoi and humans, a role separate from the ancient feminine principle.

Hecate is the goddess of death and because we all die, Hecate is a goddess for everyone. The focus on Hecate is essential for understanding the mysteries of life.- Jade Sol Luna

The Awakening of Hydra

According to Dark Goddess mysticism, the entire universe is a manifestation of pure consciousness. In manifesting the universe, this pure consciousness seems to become divided into two poles or aspects, neither of which can exist without the other.

One aspect, Light, is masculine, retains an inactive quality and remains identified with unmanifested consciousness. Light has the power to be but not the power to become or change.

The other aspect, Hecate, is feminine, active, energetic and creative. Hecate is the Great Mother of the universe, for it is from her that all form is born.

According to mystical experience, the human being is a miniature universe. All that is found in the cosmos can be found within each individual, and the same principles that apply to the universe apply in the case of the individual being.

In human beings, Hecate, the feminine aspect is called Hydra (Kundalini in India). This serpentine energy rests at the base of the spinal cord. The object of this mystic practice of awakening Hydra, is to open this astronomical energy and make it ascend through the psychic centers, the Chakras, that lie along the axis of the spine as consciousness potentials. Hydra will then unite above the crown of the head with "Sol Caelum" (refer to index page. 311) the pure conscious state of Hecate. This union is the aim of this form of mysticism: a resolution of duality into unity again, a fusion with the Absolute. By this union the mystic attains liberation while living which is considered in Dark Goddess Mysticism to be the highest experience: union of the individual with the universe.

In awakening Hydra, the state of ultimate bliss is a transcendence of dualities male-female, energy-consciousness, Sol Caelum.

Before one can begin this journey, they have to overcome the fear of death first. To stay in exalted places, one has to be completely free from fear. The state of Non-Duality is fearlessness. This is where the Goddess Hecate comes into play. Hecate is the Goddess of Death and she has the ultimate power to free a disciple from all fear. Once fear is overcome, spiritual experience is everlasting.

According to mysticism of the Dark Mother Hecate, human life embodies this flux in the aging process, the cycle of birth and rebirth, and in any experience of loss. This is applicable to all beings and their environs including angels. Because conditioned phenomena are impermanent, attachment to them becomes the cause for future suffering.

Conditioned phenomena can also be referred to as

compounded, constructed, or fabricated. This is in contrast to the unconditioned, uncompounded and unfabricated Sol Caelum, the reality that knows no change, decay or death.

Impermanence has to be understood before any devotion to the Goddess Hecate is undertaken. Her goal is to remove you from the attachments of the body. Hydra becomes awakened as fear subsides and true spiritual practice begins.

Hydra is an energy associated with empowerment and spiritual maturity. During its awakening, Hydra rises from the root Chakra up through the other Chakras or energy centers of the body, opening the door to liberation.

For some people, Hydra begins to rise slowly after years of study and spiritual work; for others, it can occur spontaneously and without any apparent logic. Hydra awakening is a powerful process that may take weeks or months, and it may or may not awaken fully.

Hecate exists in all Chakras but her home is the top portion of the Third Eye. Once Hydra pierces through the Third Eye or Luna Caelum, Hecate becomes fully conscious in the mystic. Awakening Hydra in the Third Eye is one of the goals of the mystic due to the elevated psychic experiences that follow. Once the Third Eye is permanently open, creation in it's non-dual form is realized. There is no "Light" or "Dark" for the true mystic that resides in the Third Eye, Hecate is realized in her totality, the next stage is oneness.

On the scientific level, the Third Eye is the pineal gland. The word pineal stems from the word pineus for pinecone although the pineal gland is about the size of a grain of rice. The Thyrsus is a staff tipped with a pinecone and twined with ivy, carried by Hecate (especially in cults that equated Hecate and Proserpina. Proserpina was more known for holding the Thyrsus then Hecate).

Some of these ancient key Amulets were made in silver (Diana's own metal) and have heart-shaped handles, implying, it is thought by some writers, that the affections must be prudently guarded. The key and the Thyrsus were also attributed to Hecate Proserpine, who was the guardian of the underworld and could release the spirits of the departed. The key is shown attached to a finger ring, which was a very popular form of its use. ~
William Thomas, Kate Pavitt-Birth of Humanity and Zodiac Gems p.90

Hecate represents the Goddess of the metamorphic process of spiritual death and rebirth; the most alchemistic human experience ever to be encountered. Hecate must have been the original Goddess of Hydra awakening (Kundalini) for she carries a Thyrsus (as well did Bacchus). The swirling snakes around Hecate also imply the awakening of the serpent mother Hydra and the pinecone, the pineal gland.

Whether the pinecone signifies the pineal gland or not, it is obvious that the pinecone represents the "flowering" of consciousness. The pinecone is reminiscent of the thousand petalled crown Chakra-- the Sahasrara, and the ivy represents the double-helical flow of Hydra (Kundalini) around the central channel of the spine--the sushumna. This symbol is perhaps a more ancient version of the staff of Hermes--the Caduceus, which used in alchemical and esoteric schools and now the medical industry. Hecate and Hermes both shared this symbol in Ancient Greek literature. (1) personal reference

An occult description of the Caduceus of Hermes (Mercury) is that the serpents represent positive and negative charges of Hydra (Kundalini) as it moves through the Chakras and around the spine (the staff) to the head where conscious perception occurs, the domain of Mercury the messenger. The wings of Hermes represent consciousness or Spirit. The "flow" signifies consciousness and perception--for no flow, means no life force. Spiritual evolution is an ever increasing relationship with the neutral ground between the play of opposites. The Trinity is also observable in the caduceus: the helix is the Son (matter), the staff is the Father and the wings are the Holy Ghost (tangible perception of spirit).

The staff represents the stiffened spine when Hydra passes through the central channel, but it can also represent zero-point, the neutral ground between the positive and negative charges. Astronomical overlapping being the mutual merger of two opposing energy streams; thus you could say its the place where the male and female become one (Hermekate, the merging of Hecate and Hermes). This neutral zone (staff) only comes into being through the dance of the poles/sexes/ hemispheres. The "appearance" of matter, energy and Mind from the Void is generated from this dance.

Did the Mediterranean have Chakras?

One of the well-known and notable features of Mystic philosophy is its doctrine of the seven Chakras, or spinal psychic centers. The Chakras are also the focus of many forms of holistic healing practiced today.

But did the ancient Mediterranean have any notions of the Chakras or any Chakra system? The answer is yes. Classical Mediterranean ideas about the Chakras are contained in the writings of Plato, and alluded to in the teachings of Pythagoras and in the Hermetic traditions of Western esotericism.

Plato and the Chakras

The clearest Mediterranean ideas on the Chakras come from Plato, who writes about them in his dialogue Timaeus. Basically, Plato considered the Chakras to be subtle organs that the soul, or psyche uses to relate to the gross physical body.

According to Plato's philosophy, the soul has three basic parts, or levels of expression:

Nous or Logos - This is the highest part or level of soul expression, which Plato called the psyche, or immortal soul. Its attributes are reason, wisdom and spiritual insight. It finds expression through the Crown and Brow centers.

Thymos - This is the middle level of soul expression, or what Plato called the mortal soul. Its basic attributes are passion, fight and drive. It finds expression through the middle three Chakras: the Throat, Heart and Gastric centers.

Epithymia - This is the level of desire and instinct, and is the lowest level of soul expression. It is also concerned with basic survival needs and appetites, and finds expression through the two lowest Chakras: the Generative and Root centers.

Obvious parallels can be drawn between Plato's three

levels of soul expression and the three Gunas of yogic philosophy, as well as the ego, id and superego of Freudian psychology. The correspondences are:

Nous, Logos - the Sattva Guna and the superego.
Thymos - the Rajas Guna and the ego.
Epithymia - the Tamas Guna and the id.

The Greco-Roman Chakras

Classical Greek and Roman ideas about the Chakras can be summed up as follows: (please note that the Latin names are used throughout this book)

The Crown Center

Greek: Koruphe Latin: **Vertex**

Plato said humans stand upright because the divine consciousness incarnate in their brains is physically attracted to the heavens, and to God. The crown center has also been depicted as a nimbus or halo around the heads of saints and spiritual adepts in Greece as far back as the 3rd century BCE. Hindus call it Sahasrara, or the Thousand Petaled Lotus.

The Third Eye

Greek: Enkephalos Latin: **Cerebrum**

This center Plato considered to be the seat of the psyche, or immortal soul, which the Romans called the genios or anima. In Homeric times, the heart was considered to be the seat of the soul or consciousness in man, but by Plato's and Hippocrates' day, the head or brain was seen as the seat of the soul and rational mind. The physical substance seen to embody the essence of the soul was the marrow or cerebrospinal fluid. The Brow Center and all the Chakras are rich in this sap or marrow, from which emanates their spiritual energy. As the seat of the rational mind, the Brow Center was seen to exert a controlling or restraining action on all the lower Chakras. The Sanskrit name for this Chakra, Ajna, means, "Command Center."

The Throat Center

Greek: Trachelos Latin: **Collum**

Plato called this Chakra the isthmus or boundary between the psyche, or immortal soul, and the mortal soul, or thymos. It allows for communication between the two, between the reason of the mind and the passions of the body, but forms a kind of filter or purifier to only allow refined spiritual energy to ascend to the head. The Throat Center is the psychosomatic link between mind and body. The Sanskrit name for this Chakra, Vishuddha, means, "With Purity", which is an apt description.

The Heart Center

Greek: Phrenes Latin: **Cor**

This Chakra contains the thymos, which Plato identified as the higher part of the mortal soul. This thymos is also the essence of the Vital Faculty, the heart and lungs, which concerns pneuma, the Breath or Spirit. In Homer's time, it was considered to be the seat of all thought, feeling and consciousness. By Plato's time the Heart Center had become the seat of the passions, emotions and feeling mind, whereas the Brow Center was the seat of the rational mind and soul. In Plato's system, a Midriff Partition, which manifests physically as the diaphragm, exists between the Heart Center and the three lower centers, which are concerned primarily with the body and its needs. Being the first of the Chakras that are truly concerned with spirit and the higher life of man beyond the needs of the body, a kind of spiritual rebirth takes place in the Heart Center. The Sanskrit name for this Chakra, Anahata, means, "unstruck", referring to the spiritual sounds and music heard here.

The Gastric Center, or Abdomen

Greek: Gaster Latin: **Abdomen**

Located in the Abdomen, between the diaphragm and the navel, the Gastric Center is the seat of the lower part of the mortal soul, or what Plato called the Appetitive Soul. The Appetitive Soul is the source of our appetites and desires, and says, "Feed me!" It is the seat of the Fire element, which consumes and digests food in the process of pepsis. It's also the seat of personal power, ambition and drive, which seeks to conquer all and assimilate it into oneself. The Sanskrit name for this Chakra, Manipura, means, "Jewel City", since it sparkles with the fire of a million jewels.

The Generative Center

Greek: Gonades Latin: **Genitalia**

This is the center of the Generative Faculty and procreative function. Plato says that in this center is made "the bonds of life which unite the Soul with the Body." This is the desire of life for Life, which draws a new soul into physical embodiment. Powerful forces and drives, transcending the boundaries of personal consciousness, motivate this center. The ancient Greeks considered semen to be a kind of cerebrospinal sap or spiritual essence that was passed down the spine and into the womb to produce a new life. The Sanskrit name for this Chakra, Swaddhisthana, or, "One's Own Dwelling", aptly describes it, since many, preoccupied by their sexual feelings, spend a lot of time dwelling here.

The Root Center

Greek: Hieron Osteon   Latin: **Os Sacrum**

The Greek and Latin names for this center mean, "sacred bone", since it was believed that the sacral bone was the center of the whole skeleton, and that the whole body could be regenerated from this bone. The Root Center is located at the base of the spinal column, which the ancient Greeks called Hiera Syrinx, or the "Holy Reed", or tube; this corresponds to the Sanskrit Sushumna channel. This center is the seat of consciousness in its most primitive form, which is our basic survival instincts, or a clinging on to life. The Sanskrit name for this center, Muladhara, means, "Root Support", since, energetically, this Chakra supports all the others.

Besides these seven spinal energy centers, the ancient Greeks recognized several peripheral, lesser energy centers in the hands, thighs, and knees. These parts were believed to contain a high concentration of sap or marrow, or the Radical Moisture, and hence spiritual energy as well.

Modern physiology recognizes the presence of various endocrine glands which secrete potent vital essences called hormones, located at or near the spinal energy centers. No doubt the ancient Greeks and Hindus sensed this intuitively.(2) personal reference

Hydra identified with Kundalini

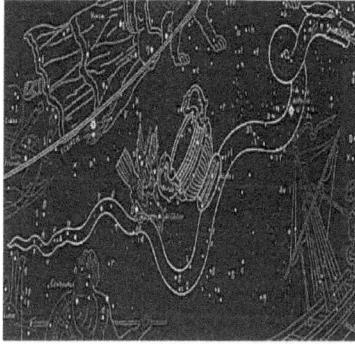

In mysticism there have been several references to the Greek Goddess Hydra being the same as Kundalini, and the Hindu God Sheshnag or Ananta.

Nyx is the Greek goddess of darkness and Hydra is the seven-headed serpent that guarded the underworld. Interestingly in Hindu Mythology we have Sheshnag, again a multi headed snake ruling the underworld (Patal) and being the seat of Lord Vishnu. Story of Sheshnag is also linked with Lord Krishna when he enters the river Yamuna to collect the ball and Sheshnag brings Him back. There is no doubt that there are close links between India and European mythology and both seem to have common origin. The connection to Hydra and Sheshnag can not be ignored.- Missing links in Jat History Vol.2

Sheshnag is known throughout India as Kundalini or Hydra fully bloomed over the head of Krishna or Narayana.

(Krishna and Sheshnag)

In Hindu Mysticism, Kundalini resides under a star called Ashlesha. The definition of Ashlesha in the Parashara is: *Serpent is the creature depicting poisonous capabilities, intensity and secret nature. Snakes also depict wisdom and Supreme form of energy of Kundalini. The Nakshatra bestows the above-mentioned qualities to the native born in it. Ashlesha people are very intense, secretive, sexual, and fierce enough to get what they want. The ambition can easily be destroying his/ her enemies, pursuing one's goal with a single mind, or exploiting the powers of Kundalini for Supreme enlightenment. If given to their negative tendencies, they can be very bad avengers and manipulators. Their inherent wisdom makes them quite adept in astrology and psychology. As Ashlesha is the home of Kundalini, this Nakshatra bestows enlightenment through discipline, undisciplined, the native falls apart.*

In Roman mysticism, this location in the sidereal

zodiac is called Hydra Palace, the "HEAD" of the Goddess Hydra (the head is placed at the tail end of Cancer). I personally prefer the term Hydra over Kundalini due to the seven heads (sometimes nine heads are used in the "Path of Hydra" if the Nodes of Astrology are brought into play) of Hydra reflecting the seven Caelums, Chakras or planes of spiritual realization that one has to transverse in order to realize the self. Even the story of Hercules cutting off the heads of Hydra can reflect the transcendence of each Caelum. Before one moves from one Caelum to another, the tie to the current Caelum needs to be severed. When a mystic is on the first plane of Saturnus Caelum, the mystic can not move on to Jove Caelum until they experience and sever their attachments to that plane. Each Caelum is a greater realization of the self.

Hydra is similar to the personality of Kundalini as well. This is based upon the fact that Kundalini can be an enormously challenging force if channeled without caution or discipline. Hydra can seize the person creating negative as opposed to positive experiences. This happens if the person has too much fear or attachments to the gross plane. This is why the guidance and personality of Hecate is necessary in order to have "real Hydra awakening." She possesses all the tools to allow the mystic to transcend fear and attachments. If fear and attachment are to strong, the negative qualities of Hydra awaking are:

1. An overload of one's nervous system with the potential to cause a break with reality, necessitating medical treatment.

2. Short or long-term disorientation where one spaces in and out of higher planes and is rendered unable to focus long enough to be able to work.

3. Sexual dysfunction: I know of several people unable to have normal relationships with their partners due to the workings of the Kundalini current in the genital areas. I have read of others with the same conditions. This usually passes in time, but I know of individuals who have been burdened with it for years.

4. Anxiety: when Kundalini becomes overwhelming, it can make one feel as though they are on the brink of losing their mind, and cause constant fear.

5. Nightly dreams where one leaves the body; in some cases a person feels as if they are being tormented by negative entities that seem too real and cause one to wake up in total fear, thinking they are doomed to experience these hellish dreams over and over.

Self-realization is the ultimate and the most desirable state to be attained, and the awakened Hydra leads to this state. However, even when Hydra is aroused and spiritual evolution is substantially hastened, there is no guarantee that Self-realization will be attained in the current lifetime. Therefore, it is encouraging to know many tangible benefits are gained even during the early states of the awakening and upward travel of Hydra.

So what is Kundalini or Hydra?

Kundalini literally means "coiled." In Indian yoga, a "corporeal energy" - an unconscious, instinctive or libidinal force, envisioned either as a goddess or else as a sleeping serpent coiled (Hydra) at the base of the spine, hence Kundalini is 'serpent power' that when awakened, awakens the individual to divine consciousness.

To awaken Hydra, the body and spirit must be prepared by mystic austerities such as meditation, invocation, and chanting. Hydra rises from the Os Sacrum Chakra up a subtle channel at the base of the spine, and from there to top of the head merging with the Vertex Chakra. The awakening is not a physical occurrence. It consists exclusively of development in consciousness. With awakening of Kundalini, our consciousness expands and we become more aware of the truth. When Kundalini or Hydra is conceived as a snake goddess, then, when it rises to the head, it unites itself with Sol Caelum (pure light). Then the mystic becomes engrossed in deep meditation and infinite bliss. The arousing of Kundalini is said to be the greatest way of attaining Divine Wisdom. Self-

Realization is equivalent to Divine Wisdom, God Realization or what ever amounts to the ultimate level of Self-Knowledge. The awakening of the Kundalini shows itself as the "awakening of inner knowledge" and brings with itself pure joy, pure knowledge and pure love.

Hydra, Chakras and Caelums

Hydra awakens the seven Chakras and is the seven headed, coiled serpent, residing in the Root Chakra, the first of the seven Chakras, the other six being the sex, navel, heart, throat, third eye and crown, in order.

All spiritual practices in the form of chanting, meditation, devotion and invocation are at best calculated as the energies that awaken this serpent-power. Spiritual practices make Hydra pass through all the succeeding Chakras beginning from the Root to the Crown, the home of Sol Caelum, the seat of Hecate Sol, the Absolute, conferring liberation on the mystic who assiduously practices mysticism or the technique of uniting Hydra with Sol Caelum.

In worldly-minded people, given to attachment of the senses, this Hydra power is sleeping because of the absence of any stimulus in the form of spiritual practice. It is the power of spiritual practice that awakens this serpent-power called Hydra. When the mystic seriously practices all the disciplines and fully awakens Hydra, they become entitled to act as a spiritual preceptor, guiding and helping others also to achieve the same end, the veils or layers enmeshing Hydra begin to be cleared and finally are torn asunder and the serpent-power is driven upward through the Chakras. This is the work of the Mystic, liberation through Hydra.

Super sensual visions appear before the mental eye of the mystic, new worlds with indescribable wonders and charms unfold themselves before the mystic, Caelum after Caelum reveal their existence and grandeur to the practitioner and the mystic gets divine knowledge, power and bliss. This power increases when Hydra pierces through Chakra after Chakra, making them bloom in all their glory which before the touch of Hydra, do not give out their powers. These Chakras emanate their divine light and fragrance and reveal divine secrets and phenomena, which lie concealed from the eyes of worldly-minded people who are asleep to their inner power.

When Hydra ascends one Chakra, the Mystic also ascends one step upward in the mystic ladder; the more Hydra travels upwards, the mystic also advances towards the goal or spiritual perfection in relation to it. When Hydra reaches Luna Caelum, the Mystic gets the vision of Personal God, and when the serpent-power reaches the last, the top center, or Sol Caelum, the mystic loses his/hers individuality in the ocean of pure unimaginable light and becomes one with Hecate Sol. He is no longer an ordinary man, not even a mystic, but a fully illumined master, having conquered the eternal and unlimited divine kingdom, a hero having won the battle against illusion, a liberated one having crossed the ocean of ignorance or the transmigratory existence, and a saint having the authority and capacity to save the other struggling souls of the relative world.

Hydra and the Mystic

The power of Hydra actually belongs to the mystic who has merged into this serpent-force. Hecate, Mother Divine, the active aspect of Power, Knowledge and Bliss, resides in the body of men and women in the form of Hydra, and the entire mystical path aims at awakening Her, and making Her unite with the Sol Caelum.

According to the mystic, the only thing to be destroyed is ignorance, and this ignorance cannot be destroyed either by study, or by work, or by any amount of physical twisting of yoga, but only by knowing one's real nature, which is Power, Knowledge and Bliss. The human race is divine, free and one with the Supreme Spirit *Hecate* always, which he forgets and identifies himself with matter, which itself is an illusory appearance and an overlapping of the spirit. Liberation is freedom from ignorance and the mystic is advised to constantly dissociate himself from all limitations and identify himself with the all-pervading, non-dual, blissful, peaceful, homogeneous spirit or Sol Caelum. When Hecate descends into the mystic, the experiences become intensified, the false self is blown out completely. This is the real death of Hecate. Just as a drop of water left on a frying pan is immediately sucked and vanishes from cognition, the individual consciousness is sucked in by the Universal Consciousness of Hecate and is absorbed in it. According to mystical experience there cannot be real liberation in a state of multiplicity, and the state of complete "Oneness" is the goal to be aspired for, towards which alone the entire creation is slowly moving on.

Hydra, Kundalini, Sheshnag
Plates

"The Tantric age that flourished in India was destroyed by Christianity in Greece and Rome. The merging of Hydra, Kundalini and Sheshnag did not fully mature in the west in our modern era but this does not mean that this is not so."-Krishnamuti Gopal.

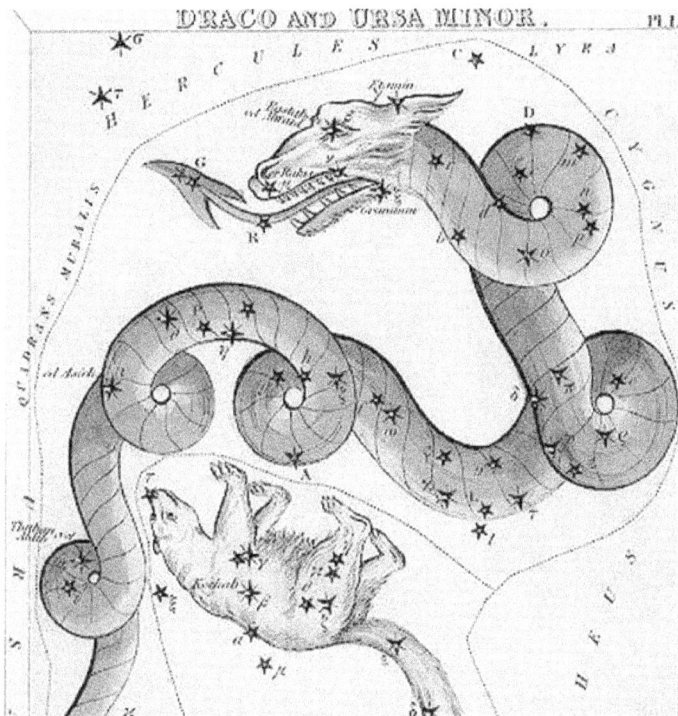

(Constellation Hydra)

(Hecate Triceps) Venetia 1556

(Hydra and seven headed Lion) St.Josephene

(Hercules and Hydra) Learna 34 B.C

beast of Babylon (equated with Hydra in Christian literature) Montana Press
1977

Vishnu and Sheshnag-Hari Ashok 1967

Harlot on Hydra (Compendium Maleficarum 1600's)

Lord Ganesh and Sheshnag (Hydra) statue Khajuraho

(Hecate flanked by serpents, Hydra power)

(Coiled Serpent) Kali Temple Calighat

Yogi and Hydra, picture Magdalina

Vishnu and Sheshnag (Hydra) Oryssa village

Whore of Babylon riding the beast of the apocalypse, HYDRA.
(Apacolyto 1955)

Buddha with fully bloomed Hydra - Thailand

The Essence of Awakening Hydra

(What can not be understood by the intellect will be absorbed by the sub-conscious. This may require at least three reads for proper understanding. As the mind slows down the subconscious and the Third Eye opens and receives. page 47-65)

The goal of awakening Hydra is the process by which the human spirit is brought into near and conscious communion with Hecate. When Hydra starts to awaken we realize our connection to the Divine, in the end we realize there is no separation. "Awakening Hydra" is that process by which the identity of the two "Self and God " is realized as **one** by the mystic. It is so realized because the Spirit has then pierced through the veil of duality which as mind and matter obscures this knowledge from itself. The means by which this is achieved is the spiritual process which liberates the spirit from ignorance. There is no force equal in strength to ignorance, and no power greater to destroy that force than Hecate. From the standpoint of a Hecate devotee, spiritual practice in the sense of a final union is inapplicable, for union implies a dualism of the Divine and human spirit. In such case, it denotes the process rather than the result. When the two are regarded as distinct, spiritual practice may apply to both. A person who practices mysticism or occultism is called a mystic. All are not competent to attempt the awakening of Hydra; only a very few are. One must, in this or in other lives, have gone through great mystical practice, selfless service and ritualistic observances, without attachment to the actions or their fruits, and devotional worship, and obtained the fruit thereof, a pure mind. A person may have a pure mind in this sense, and yet be wholly incapable of mystical devotion. Very few persons indeed are competent for mystical experience in its higher form. The majority should seek their advancement along the path of religion as mystical practices are for those longing for the mystical experience of the Caelums.

All the spiritual worlds are within Hecate and so is the Supreme Sol Caelum. The body is a shadow of Mother Hecate and may be divided into two main parts, namely, the head and trunk on the one hand, and the legs on the other. In the human being, the center of the body is between these two, at the base of the spine where the legs begin. Supporting the trunk and throughout the whole body there is the spinal cord. This is the axis of the body, just as Mount Olympus is the axis of the earth. Hence, man's spine is related to Mount Olympus, the axis-staff, the body the mount and Olympus representing the enlightened Vertex Chakra. The legs and feet are gross which show less signs of consciousness than the trunk with its spinal white and grey matter (index); which the trunk itself is greatly subordinate in this respect to the head containing the organ of mind, or physical brain, with its white and grey matter. The positions of the white and grey matter in the head and spinal column respectively are reversed. The body and legs below the center are the seven lower or nether worlds upheld by the sustaining powers of the universe. From the center upwards, consciousness more freely manifests through the spinal and cerebral centers. Here there are the seven upper regions or Caelums, namely, Saturnus Caelum, Jove Caelum, Mavors Caelum, Venus Caelum, Mercurius Caelum, Luna Caelum and Sol Caelum correspond with the six centers; five in the trunk, the sixth in the lower cerebral center; and the seventh in the upper brain or Sol Caelum, the abode of the Supreme form of Hecate.

The six centers are: the Os Sacrum Chakra situated at the base of the spinal column in a position midway in the perineum between the root of the genitals and the anus; above it, in the region of the genitals, abdomen, heart, chest and throat, and in the forehead between the two eyes, are the Sex, Navel, Heart, Throat and Third Eye Chakras respectively. These are the chief centers. The seventh region beyond the Chakras is the upper brain, the highest center of manifestation of consciousness in the body and therefore, the abode of the Supreme form of Hecate. When it is said to be the "abode", it is not meant that the Supreme is there placed in the sense of our "placing", namely, it is there and not elsewhere! The Supreme is never localized, whilst its manifestations are. It is everywhere both within and without the body, but it is said to be in the Vertex Chakra, because it is there that the Supreme form of Hecate Sol is realized. This must be so because consciousness is realized by entering in and passing through the higher manifestation of mind. Thus the cerebrum is the center of mind, and the five lower Chakras are the centers of the five elements in relation to the mind; the Collum Chakra of Ether, Cor Chakra of Wind, Abdomen Chakra of Fire, Genitalia Chakra of Water, and the Os Sacrum Chakra of Earth.

In short, the human being as a microcosm is the all-pervading Spirit (which most purely manifests in the Vertex Chakra) vehicled by Hecate in the form of mind and matter, the centers of which are the sixth and following five Chakras respectively.

The six Chakras have been identified with the following plexuses commencing from the lowest, the Os Sacrum Chakra; the sacrococcygeal plexus, the sacral plexus, the Abdomen, (which forms the great junction of the right and left sympathetic chains Ida and Pingala with the cerebro-spinal axis). Connected with this is the lumbar plexus. Then follows the cardiac plexus (Cor Chakra), laryngeal plexus, and lastly the cerebrum or cerebellum with its two lobes. Above this is the middle cerebrum, and finally, the Vertex Chakra or upper cerebrum. The six Chakras themselves are vital centers within the spinal column in the white and grey matter there. They may, however, and probably do, influence and govern the gross tract outside the spine in the bodily region lateral to, and co-extensive with, that section of the spinal column in which a particular center is situated. The Chakras are centers of Hecate as vital force. In other words these are centers of the great goddess manifested by breath in the living body, the presiding Goddess of which are names for the Universal Consciousness as it manifests in the form of those centers. The Chakras are not perceptible to the gross senses. Even if they were perceptible in the living body which they help to organize, they disappear with the disintegration of organism at death.

The petals of the lotuses vary, being 4, 6, 10, 12, 16 and 2 respectively, commencing from the Os Sacrum Chakra and ending with cerebrum.

But why, it may be asked, do the petals vary in number? Why, for instance, are there 4 in the Os Sacrum Chakra and 6 in the Genitalia Chakra? The answer given is that the number of petals in any Chakra is determined by the number and position of the Nadis (index) or spiritual nerves around that Chakra. Thus, four Nadis surrounding and passing through the vital movements of the Os Sacrum Chakra, give it the appearance of a lotus of four petals which are thus configurations made by the positions of Nadis at any particular center. The latter are gross physical nerves. But the former, here spoken of, are called spiritual nerves and are subtle channels along which the breath currents flow. The term Nadi comes from the root Nad which means motion. The body is filled with an uncountable number of Nadis. If they were revealed to the eye, the body would present the appearance of a highly-complicated chart of ocean currents. Superficially the water seems one and the same. But examination shows that it is moving with varying degrees of force in all directions. All these lotuses exist in the spinal columns.

The spinal column is the flow of all current. Western anatomy divides it into five regions; and it is to be noted in corroboration of the theory here expounded that these correspond with the regions in which the five Chakras are situated. The central spinal system comprises the brain or encephalon contained within the skull; as also the spinal cord extending from the upper border of the Atlas below the cerebellum and descending to the second lumbar vertebra where it tapers to a point called the filum terminale. Within the spine is the cord, a compound of grey and white brain matter, in which are the five lower Chakras. It is noteworthy that the filum terminale was formerly thought to be a mere fibrous cord, an unsuitable vehicle, one might think, for the Os Sacrum Chakra and the power of Hydra. More recent microscopic investigations have, however, disclosed the existence of highly sensitive grey matter in the filum terminale which represents the position of the Os Sacrum Chakra. According to Western science, the spinal cord is not merely a conductor between the periphery and the centers of sensation and volition, but is also an independent center or group of centers. The Sushumna is a Nadi in the center of the spinal column. Its base is called "Gate of liberation." As regards the physiological relations of the Chakras all that can be said with any degree of certainty is that the four above the Os Sacrum Chakra have relation to the genito-excretory, digestive, cardiac and respiratory functions and that the two upper centers, the cerebrum (with associated Chakras) and the Vertex denote various forms of its cerebral activity ending in the repose of "Pure Consciousness." Consciousness is gained through mystical practice. The Nadis of each side Ida and Pingala are the left and right sympathetic cords crossing the central column from one side to the other, making at the cerebrum with the Sushumna a threefold knot called Trivia (a form of Hecate); which is said to be the spot in the Medulla where the sympathetic cords join together and whence they take their origin—these Nadis together with the two lobed cerebrum Chakra and the Sushumna forming the figure of the Caduceus of the God Mercury which is said by some to represent them.

How is it that the rousing of Hydra effects the state of liberation and spiritual experience which is alleged?

In the first place, there are two main lines of spirituality known to Hecate as the right and left hand path (Hecate supports both paths); and there is a marked difference between the two. The Left-Hand Path and Right-Hand Path are a dichotomy between two opposing belief systems, whose meanings have varied over time. The distinction is generally used by self-proclaimed followers of the "Left-Hand Path." Opponents often argue that these definitions improperly divide belief systems (a mislabeled or false dichotomy), or claim that many Left-Hand beliefs are illegitimate.

Modern definitions of "Right-Hand Path" elevate spirituality, the strict observance of moral codes, and the worship of Olympian deities or God as one. The intent of "Right-Hand Path" belief systems is to attain proximity to divinity through actions of purity. Conversely, the "Left-Hand Path" belief systems value the advancement and preservation of the self, as well as the pursuit of physical goals. These goals are often achieved either by seeking the guidance of one or more deities (underworld deities) via ritualistic practices, or more commonly, via non-theistic uses of instincts and logic.

Although all sects value proximity to the divine, most followers of Left-Hand Path belief systems seek to merge into these divinities themselves. The goal of the "Left Handed Practitioner" is **power** and the "Right Hand Practitioner" is **purity**. The "Left Handed Practitioner" embraces the five unacceptables (mentioned in chapter 6) to achieve their goal.

If liberation is sought without desire for union through Hydra, then, such spiritual paths are not necessary; for, Liberation may be obtained by Pure wisdom through detachment, the exercise and then the stilling of the mind, without any rousing of the central Bodily-power of Hydra at all. Instead of setting out in and from the world to unite with God, to attain this result, detaches himself from the world.

If the Ultimate Reality is the One which exists in two aspects of quiescent enjoyment of the Self, and of liberation from all form and active enjoyment of objects, that is, as pure spirit, then a complete union with Reality demands such unity in both of its aspects. When rightly apprehended and practiced, there is truth in the doctrine which teaches that man should make the best of both worlds. There is no real incompatibility between the two, provided action is taken in conformity with the universal law of manifestation. It is held to be false teaching that happiness hereafter can only be had by absence of enjoyment now (emphasized in Christianity), or in deliberately sought for suffering and mortification. It is the one Hecate who is the Supreme Blissful Experience and who appears in the form of man/woman with a life of mingled pleasure and pain. Both happiness here and the bliss of Liberation here and hereafter may be attained. This will be achieved by making every human function, without exception, a religious act of sacrifice and worship (experiencing Hecate in everything). In ancient Roman/Greco ritual, enjoyment by way of food and drink was preceded and accompanied by ceremonial sacrifice and ritual. Such enjoyment was the fruit of the sacrifice and the gift of the Gods. At a higher stage in the life of a mystic, it is offered to the One from whom all gifts come and of whom the Gods are inferior limited forms. But this offering also involves a dualism from which the highest (Non-Duality) mystic is free. Here the individual life and the worldly life are known as one. And the mystic, when eating or drinking or fulfilling any other of the natural functions of the body, does so, saying and feeling "Hecate is in everything." It is not merely the separate individual who thus acts and enjoys. It is Hecate who does so in and through the worshiper. Such a one recognizes, as has been said, that his life and the play of all its activities are not a thing apart, to be held and pursued egotistically for its and his own separate sake, as though enjoyment was something to be filched from life by his own unaided strength and with a sense of separateness; but his life and all its activities are conceived as part of the Divine action in Nature (Hecate) manifesting and operating in the form of human beings. He realizes in the pulsating beat of his heart the rhythm which throbs through and is the song of the Universal Consciousness. To neglect or to deny the needs of the body, to think of it as something not divine, is to neglect and deny the greater life of which it is a part, and to falsify the great doctrine of the unity of all and of the ultimate identity of Matter and Spirit. Governed by such a concept, even the lowliest physical needs take on a astronomical significance. The body is Hecate; its needs are Hecate's needs. When the human being enjoys, it is Hecate who enjoys through him. In all he sees and does, it is the Mother who looks and acts, His eyes and hands are Hers. The whole body and all its functions are Her manifestations. To fully realize Her as such is to perfect this particular manifestation of Hers which is the self. Human beings when seeking to be the master of themselves, seeks so on all the planes physical, mental and spiritual nor can they be severed, for they are all related, being but differing aspects of the one all-pervading Consciousness. Who, it may be asked, is the more divine; he who neglects and spurns the body or mind that he may attain some fancied spiritual superiority, or he who rightly cherishes both as forms of the one Spirit which they clothe? Realization is more speedily and truly attained by discerning Spirit in and as all being and its activities, then by fleeing from and casting these aside as being either unspiritual or illusory and impediments in the path. When the Mother Hecate is seen in all things, She is at length realized as She who is beyond them all.

These general principles have their more frequent application in the life of the world before entrance on the path of mysticism. The mysticism here described is, however, also an application of these same principles, in so far as it is claimed that thereby both enjoyment and liberation are attained.

Hecate in Two Forms

There is polarization of Hecate into two forms— inactive and active. In the mind or experience this polarization is patent to reflection; namely, the polarity between pure Power and the Stress which is involved in it. This Stress or Power develops the mind through an infinity of forms and changes in the pure unbounded Ether of Consciousness. This analysis exhibits the primordial power of Hecate in the same two polar forms as before, inactive and active. Here the polarity is most fundamental and approaches absoluteness, though of course, it is to be remembered that there is no absolute rest except in Sol Caelum. Astronomical energy is in an equilibrium which is relative and not absolute.

Passing from mind, let us take matter. The atom of modern science has ceased to be an atom in the sense of an indivisible unit of matter. According to the electron theory, the atom is a miniature universe resembling our solar system. At the center of this atomic system we have a charge of positive electricity around which a cloud of negative charges called electrons revolve. The positive charges hold each other in check so that the atom is in a condition of equilibrated energy and does not ordinarily break up, though it may do so on the dissociation which is the characteristic of all matter, but which is so clearly manifest in the radioactivity of radium. We have thus here again, a positive charge at rest at the center, and negative charges in motion round about the center. What is thus said about the atom applies to the whole astronomical system and universe. In the world-system, the planets revolve around the Sun, and that system itself is probably (taken as a whole) a moving mass around some other relatively inactive center, until we arrive at Sol Caelum which is the point of Absolute Rest, around which all forms revolve and by which all are maintained. Similarly, in the tissues of the living body, the operative energy is polarized into two forms of energy—anabolic and catabolic, the one tending to change and the other to conserve the tissues; the actual condition of the tissues being simply the resultant of these two co-existent or concurrent activities.

In short, Hecate, when manifesting, divides herself into two polar aspects—inactive and active—which implies that you cannot have it in an active form without at the same time having it in an inactive form, much like the poles of a magnet. In any given sphere of activity of force, we must have, according to the astronomical principle of an inactive back-ground—

Hydra at rest or "coiled." This scientific truth is within Mother Hecate moving as the Kinetic power who awakens the devotee to Sol Caelum which is the inactive state of pure light which is actionless, the Universal Mother being all activity.

The Astronomical Hecate is the collectivity in relation to which Hydra in particular bodies is the individual power. The body is, as I have stated, a microcosm. In the living body there is, therefore, the same polarization of which I have spoken. From the Great Mother Hecate, the universe has sprung. In Her Supreme Form She is at rest, coiled round and one with Sol Caelum.

(Hecate symbolized as the snake and the egg symbolizes Sol Caelum)

She is then at rest. She next uncoils herself to manifest. Here the four coils of which mysticism speaks are the four worlds (traditionally listed at three worlds excluding Sol Caelum, the image portrays all four, the Gross, Subtle, Mental and Sol Caelum). She is thus moving, and continues even after creation to evolve what she created. For, as they are born of movement, they continue to move. The whole world is moving in perfect consciousness. Hecate thus continues creatively acting until She has evolved the last soul. First She creates mind, and then matter. This latter becomes more and more dense. Air density associated with the maximum velocity of gravity; Fire density associated with the velocity of light; Water or fluid density associated with molecular velocity and the equatorial velocity of the earth's rotation; and Earth density, that of basalt associated with the velocity of sound. However, it is plain that the elements represent an increasing density of matter until it reaches its three dimensional solid form. When Hecate has created this last, what is there further for Her to do? Nothing. She therefore then again rests. At rest, again, means that She assumes an inactive form. Hecate, however, is never exhausted, that is, emptied into any of its forms. Therefore, Hydra, at this point is, as it were, the power left over after the earth element, the last of the elements, has been created. We have thus Great Hydra at rest in Sol Caelum, the point of absolute rest; and then the body in which the relative inactive center is Hydra at rest, and around this center the whole of the bodily forces move. They are power, and so is Hydra. The difference between the two is that they are powers in specific differentiated forms in movement; and Hydra is undifferentiated, residual power at rest, that is, coiled. She is coiled in the Os Sacrum Chakra, which means 'fundamental support', and which is at the same time the seat of earth or last solid matter and of the residual power or Hydra. The body may, therefore, be compared to a magnet with two poles. The Os Sacrum Chakra, in so far as it is the seat of Hydra, a comparatively gross form of power, is the inactive pole in relation to the rest of the body which is active. The working that is the body necessarily presupposes and finds such an inactive support, hence the name "Os Sacrum Chakra." In sense, the inactive power at the Os Sacrum Chakra is necessarily coexistent with the creating and evolving power of the body; because the active aspect or pole can never be without its inactive counterpart. In another sense, it is the residual power left over after such operation.

The Effect of Hydra

What then happens in the accomplishment of awakening Hydra? This inactive power is affected by breathing and other mystical processes and becomes active. Thus, when Hydra becomes active, Hydra strives to unite with Sol Caelum in the Vertex Chakra. The two poles are united in one and there is the state of consciousness and the mystic enters the divine spiritual state of the Caelums (Hindu Samadhi). The polarization, of course, takes place in consciousness. The body actually continues to exist as an object of observation to others. It continues its organic life. But man's consciousness of his body and all other objects is withdrawn because the mind has ceased so far as his consciousness is concerned, the function having been withdrawn into its ground which is consciousness.

How is the body sustained? In the first place, though

the power of Hydra is the inactive center of the whole body as a complete conscious organism, yet each of the parts of the body and their constituent cells have their own inactive centers which uphold such parts or cells. Next, the theory of mystics is that Hydra ascends and that the body, as a complete organism, is maintained by the spiritual bliss which flows from the union of Hydra and Sol Caelum in the Vertex Chakra. This bliss is an ejection of power generated by their union. The potential power of Hydra becomes only partly and not wholly converted into kinetic power; and yet since the power of Hydra—even as given in the Os Sacrum Chakra—is an infinitude, it is not depleted; the power of Hydra always remains unexhausted. In this case, the active equivalent is a partial conversion of one mode of energy into another. If, however, the coiled power of Hydra at the Os Sacrum Chakra became absolutely uncoiled, there would result the dissolution of the three bodies—gross, subtle and causal, and consequently, bodiless Liberation—because the inactive background in relation to a particular form of existence would, according to this hypothesis, have wholly given way. The body becomes cold as a corpse as the power leaves it, not due to the depletion or privation of the static power at the Os Sacrum Chakra but to the concentration or convergence of the active power ordinarily diffused over the whole body, so that the active equivalent which is set up against the inactive background of Hydra is only the diffused fivefold life force gathered home—withdrawn from the other tissues of the body and concentrated along the axis. Thus, ordinarily, the active equivalent is the life force diffused over all the tissues: in mysticism, it is converged along the axis, the inactive equivalent of Hydra enduring in both cases. Some part of the already available active life force is made to act at the base of the axis in a suitable manner, by which means the basal center or the Os Sacrum Chakra becomes, as it were, oversaturated and reacts on the whole diffused active power of the body by withdrawing it from the tissues and converging it along the line of the axis. In this way, the diffused active equivalent becomes the converged active equivalent along the axis. What, according to this view, ascends is not the whole power but an eject like condensed lightning, which at length reaches Sol Caelum. There the Central Power which upholds the individual world-Consciousness is merged in the Supreme Consciousness of Hecate. The limited consciousness, transcending the passing concepts of worldly life, directly intuits the unchanging Reality which underlies the whole phenomenal flow. When Hydra sleeps in the Os Sacrum Chakra, man is awake to the world; when she awakes to unite, and does unite, with the Supreme inactive Consciousness which is Sol Caelum, then consciousness is asleep to the world and is one with the Light of all things.

The main principle is that when awakened, Hydra, ceases to be an inactive Power which sustains the world-consciousness, the content of which is held only so long as She sleeps; and when once set in movement is drawn to that other inactive center in the Thousand-Vertex Chakra which is Herself in union with the oneness or the consciousness of ecstasy beyond the world of form. When Hydra sleeps, man is awake to this world. When She wakes, he sleeps— that is, loses all consciousness of the world and enters the Caelums. In mysticism, he passes beyond to the formless Consciousness of Sol Caelum.

Glory to Mother Hecate, who through Her Infinite Grace and Power, kindly leads her devotee from Chakra to Chakra and illumines Hydra!

The Chakras and Hecate

"When Hydra is awakened she moves on from the Os Sacrum Chakra to the Vertex Chakra. At every center to which the mystic directs Hydra, he experiences a special form of Bliss and gains special psychic powers and knowledge. He enjoys the Supreme Bliss when Hydra is taken to the Vertex Chakra."

The Os Sacrum Chakra

The Os Sacrum Chakra is located at the base of the spinal column. It lies between the origin of the reproductory organ and the anus. Two fingers above the anus and about two fingers below the genitals, four fingers in width is the space where the Os Sacrum Chakra is situated. This is the support Chakra. Hydra, which gives power and energy to all the Chakras, lies at this Chakra. Hence, the Os Sacrum Chakra , which is the support of all is called the Root or Support Chakra.

From the Os Sacrum Chakra four important Nadis emanate which appear as petals of a lotus. The center of this Chakra is called cupid (desire) and it is worshiped by powerful mystics. Here Hydra lies dormant. Brimo is the Goddess of the Os Sacrum Chakra and Saturn is the overlord. It is through Brimo, the serpent form of Hecate, that Hydra is awakened. The mystic, who has penetrated the Os

Sacrum Chakra through spiritual devotion, has conquered illusion. He has no fear of death.

The wise Mystic, who concentrates and meditates on the Os Sacrum Chakra, acquires full knowledge of Hydra and the means to awaken it. When Hydra is awakened, he gets the power of non-duality. He can control the breath and mind. All bad karma is destroyed. He acquires knowledge of the past, present and future. He enjoys the natural Bliss of Saturnus Caelum.

Os Sacrum Chakra Facts:

- The first Chakra governs eating, the need for shelter, warmth, and comfort and the desire to feel protected.

- A well-balanced root Chakra results in a feeling of calm and an aura of quiet strength and confidence.

- In your body, the first Chakra governs the bones, blood, immune system, colon, rectum, legs, and feet.

- An apt image for the first Chakra is a plant or tree rooted firmly in Mother Earth.

- The root Chakra vibrates with the color red.

- The Root Chakra's mission statement is: I want, I need.

Maintaining a balanced foundation is an ongoing and sometimes challenging process. Life is ever changing, and you must be able to go with the flow, bending like the branches of a tree in an unpredictable wind. Because it is impossible to control your external environment, you must concentrate on creating an inner environment that is both solid and flexible.

Brimo is the form of Hecate that awakens Hydra

The Dark Goddess is our guide, the high priestess of mystic ritual of self-transcendence. As this inner or "mystic death", Brimo appears in her fierce form carrying the athame which removes the ego, her power in the underworld reveals our past lives and their sorrows. She opens the door to liberation and represents the eternal death of the outer world that is the inner peace of eternity.

Hecate Brimo's power is awakening Hydra, the power of action behind the entire inner mystic process, which renders us from non-being to being, from the many to the one, from the not-self to the Self, and from darkness to light. This occurs through the awakening of Hydra in the Os Sacrum Chakra and the movement through the Chakras. Hydra traces our journey back through the astronomical elements to our true Self beyond all manifestation, through the mergence of all factors of existence in the spiritual heart.

Hecate Brimo's power over death reverses the process of creation, taking us from multiplicity to unity. This is our spiritual rebirth as a Divine being of pure consciousness and bliss after the dissolution of the elements, sense organs, body and mind that we usually identify ourselves with.

Invocation:

While concentrating on the Os Sacrum Chakra, chant BRIMO, allow the buzz of the "M" to be felt inside the Chakra.

Genitalia Chakra

The Genitalia Chakra is located within the Sushumna Nadi at the root of the reproductive organ. This corresponds to Jove Caelum. This Chakra has control over the lower abdomen and kidneys in the physical body. The elements of this Chakra is water. Within this Chakra there is a space like a crescent moon or the form of a conch shell. The presiding deity is Hecate Triceps and Jove is the overlord. The color of the Chakra is pure blood-like red or vermilion. From this center six Nadis emanate, which appear like the petals of a lotus.

He who concentrates on this Chakra and meditates with the Goddess Triceps opens the door to ecstasy. He has perfect control over the water element. He gets many psychic powers, intuitional knowledge and perfect control over his senses. The Mystic becomes the conqueror of death.

Genitalia Chakra Facts:

- The second Chakra creates your passion for life, celebrating good times, good sex and good food.

- A well-balanced second Chakra will result in a satisfied appetite for
life, physical gratification, emotional fulfillment and creative expression.

- In your body, the second Chakra governs the sexual and reproductive organs, the bladder, and part of the lower intestine.

- An apt image for the second Chakra is a warm, exciting fireplace in your belly.

- The second Chakra vibrates with the color vermilion.

- The second Chakra's mission statement is: I feel, I sense, I discover.

When your second Chakra is unbalanced, you might have the tendency of avoiding, controlling or ignoring your feelings. Or you might even disconnect from the sensual altogether, severing yourself from your sense and your feelings, and living your life in your head. If the imbalance is great enough, you could experience self-denial, self-rejection, and self-deprivation. Shadows can envelope your life, putting to an end all spontaneity, pleasure, and joy.

At its very worst, an imbalanced second Chakra can lead to anorexia, bulimia, addiction, sexual dysfunction and depression.

Hecate Triceps Holds the power of ecstacy

After Brimo comes Hecate Triceps, closely resembling Brimo in her appearance. Mother Triceps holds the capacity to save us, to deliver us from ignorance to enlightenment. Yet more than this, on a astronomical level she is the power of both ascent and descent, through which the soul aspires upwards to divinity, on one hand, and through which Divine grace flows down from above, on the other.

The astronomical existence consists of a series of levels, layers which form the different worlds and realms of experience. Mother Triceps provides us the knowledge of each plane of existence, guiding us in moving up or down from one to the other. Triceps gives us the skill in both the ascent of higher forces from below and their descent as grace from above.

More specifically, Mother Triceps initiates the upward movement of energy that is the main action of Hecate's power, our ascent to the Supreme or movement up through the Chakras. She is the inner guide and high priestess of our spiritual ascent. Once awakened within us, Brimo becomes Triceps and emanates her out of herself to take us forward. Mother Triceps delivers us from obstacles, particularly from drowning in the ocean of ignorance and negative emotion.

Invocation:

While concentrating on the Genitalia Chakra, chant TRICEPS, allow the buzz of the I "EE" to be felt inside the Chakra.

The Abdomen Chakra

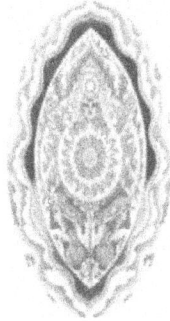

The Abdomen Chakra is the third Chakra from the Root. It is located within the region of the navel. The navel is the corresponding center in the physical body and has control over the liver and stomach. This is a very important center. From this Chakra emanates ten Nadis which appear like the petals of a lotus. The Chakra is the color of dark clouds on the outside and yellow on the inside. Within there is a space triangular in form. This is the realm of Fire. The presiding deity is Hecate Scorpio and the God Mars is the overlord. This Chakra corresponds to Mavors Caelum and the Abdomen in the physical body.

The Mystic who concentrates on this Chakra can acquire hidden mystical secrets and will be free from all diseases. He has the power of fire.

Abdomen Chakra Facts:

- The third Chakra rules your self-direction, self-control, personal will and physical energy.

- A well-balanced third Chakra results in high self-esteem and the ability to accept responsibility for yourself, while assuming personal authority over your life.

- In your body, the third Chakra governs the stomach, pancreas, upper intestines, gallbladder, liver, and lower back.

- An apt image for the third Chakra is the bright Sun.

- The Abdomen Chakra vibrates with the color yellow.

- The Abdomen Chakra's mission statement is: I choose, I intend, I will.

Physically, an imbalanced Abdomen Chakra can result in digestive problems, ulcers, irritable colon, gallbladder problems, excessive weight around your middle and loss of appetite. Spiritually, you can fail to live your own truth and to be who you are really meant to be.

Codependency-making decisions or taking actions based on the belief that pleasing others is more important than pleasing yourself is among the negative emotional consequences of imbalanced personal sovereignty. So are fear of rejection, disapproval or abandonment, as well as depression, addiction, and suppressed anger.

The Abdomen Chakra can also be imbalanced in the other direction: You can have too much sovereignty. When that happens, you can become narrow-minded, relentless and unyielding. Extremely overcompensating people can be intimidating, overbearing, and insensitive. Although society actually honors some of these aggressive qualities, they produce workaholism, strained relationships and the inability to slow down or relax.

Hecate Scorpio, Queen of Fire

Third of the Chakra Goddesses is Hecate Scorpio, the fiery Goddess of beauty and delight. Such beauty is not an aspect of the outer Venus energy through which people seek enjoyment, happiness and prosperity in the external world. She is the beauty of Hecate, the beauty and delight inherent in Hecate or the inner mystical process. Once we have gone through Brimo and been lead by Mother Triceps upward, we rediscover beauty and delight as an inner power through Hecate Scorpio, which is embodied as the principle in the Vertex Chakra.

The spiritual path is not just about renunciation, austerity, detachment, denial, death or deprivation. It is about seeking a higher beauty and delight than what can be found in the forms, objects, events and experiences of the outer world. This quest for inner delight leads us to Hecate Scorpio.

Hecate Scorpio is the attractive or magnetic force of the Divine Mother Hecate, which draws us in love and aspiration back to our true nature. Without this inner attraction the spiritual path would be dry, pessimistic and constricting. We can only give up something we enjoy externally for something more beautiful within. Actually it is the inner beauty which draws us to the external forms. We usually need some suffering or disappointment in the outer world to turn us within, unless we discover that inner attraction we cannot continue in our quest for eternal bliss.

Hecate Scorpio is the attractive power of Hecate, differing her electrical force. She is the power of immortal life. We can only give up one thing for something better, even in the external world. The same law is true of the internal world. Unless we have a sense of the greater Divine bliss, we cannot go far on our path. Hecate Scorpio provides this attraction for us, the inner bliss or nectar to nourish and inspire us along the way.

Invocation:

While concentrating on the Abdomen Chakra, chant SCORPIO, allow the buzz of the "O" to be felt inside the Chakra.

The Cor Chakra

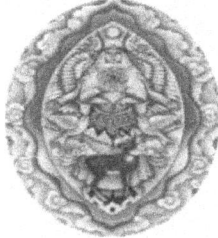

The Cor Chakra is situated in the heart center. It has control over the power of the heart. It corresponds to the Cardiac Plexus in the physical body. This corresponds to Venus Caelum. This Chakra is of deep red color. Within this Chakra there is a hexagonal space of smoke or deep black color or the color of collyrium (used for the eyes). This Chakra is the center of Wind. The presiding deity is Hecate Lucifera, the most worshiped form of Hecate and the overlord is Venus. The divine sound of the sirens is heard at this center. When you meditate on this center for a long time, you can distinctly hear their music.

He who meditates on this Chakra has full control over the wind element. He receives divine love and all other pure qualities.

Cor Chakra Facts:

- The heart Chakra rules your compassion, forgiveness, generosity and love.

- A well-balanced fourth Chakra will result in stimulating your highest
ideals and desires, and leave you feeling positive and nurturing.

- In your body, the fourth Chakra governs the heart, circulation, breasts, and arteries.

- An apt image for the fourth Chakra is an open doorway.

- The heart Chakra vibrates with the color blood red.

- The heart Chakra's mission statement is: I give, I care, I love.

When your heart Chakra is balanced, you non-judgmentally accept yourself and others. You recognize beauty-in yourself and in everyone-while overlooking weaknesses. It is because of a balanced fourth Chakra that you are kind and forgiving, as well as quick to pardon. You are also tolerant, optimistic, resourceful and humorous.

If your heart Chakra is off balance or shut down, you might have a tendency to run away from intimacy. You might even intentionally push otherwise loving and lovable people away from you. Without this sense of connection, you become critical, suspicious and defensive. Paranoia becomes a real possibility. If your heart center shuts down completely, you may be inclined toward secrecy, betrayal and addictions.

By closing your heart, you continue to push people away, who in response reject you again, seemingly validating your initial feeling to seal yourself off. Again and again you pull back. Again and again you're pushed away. It's a self-fulfilling prophecy. Your heart becomes more closed and you become more isolated.

A heart Chakra imbalanced in the opposite direction-too wide open-causes problems too. You can become too empathic, too easily picking up on the anger or depression of others. You live at the mercy of the moods and feelings of those around you. This can be psychically and physically draining.

Hecate Lucifera holds the power of clarity

Lucifera represents the ruling power of Hecate, the Mother's executive force governing the entire universe, the movement of time and the orientation of objects in space. Her power of making clear or evident allows all grace to manifest. As we move within, we go beyond outer human realms, even the forces of nature and come into contact with this great ruling power of the Mother, through which alone all things can operate.

Coming under the Goddess's power and vision, she restructures our view of the world according to her wisdom and grace, giving us a sense of freedom, expanse and joy in our actions, magnifying the influence of Hecate. She creates space and freedom within us, connecting us to our soul's mastery of the world processes.

Invocation:

While concentrating on the Cor Chakra, chant Lucifera, allow the buzz of the U "OO" to be felt inside the Chakra.

The Collum Chakra

The Collum Chakra is situated within the Sushumna Nadi at the base of the throat. This corresponds to Mercurius Caelum. It is the center of the ether element. This Chakra is of pure blue color. The presiding Goddess is Hecate Trivia, and the Overlord is Mercury. This Chakra corresponds to Laryngeal plexus in the physical body. He who meditates here will experience longevity. He attains the highest success. He gets the full knowledge by meditating on this Chakra. He becomes a wisdom master (who knows the past, the present and the future).

Collum Chakra Facts:

- The fifth Chakra rules your communication, creativity, connection and personal intention.

- A well-balanced fifth Chakra awakens in you the truth that your life is built on your words, thoughts, beliefs and ideas.

- In your body, the fifth Chakra governs throat, thyroid, trachea,
  esophagus, neck, mouth, teeth, and ears.

- An apt image for the fifth Chakra is a chimney.

- The Collum Chakra vibrates with blue color.

- The Collum Chakra's mission statement is: I express, I listen, I communicate.

A well-balanced Collum Chakra enables your expression to act as a three-way psychic radio. The first band, which activates your speaking and listening abilities, also governs all forms of creativity and awakens your ability to connect with others. The second band establishes mental and telepathic rapport with others, sending and receiving thoughts and feelings, especially from those who are on the same wavelength as you. Finally, the third band tunes in to your own inner voice, allowing you to pick up on your intention and to ask for and receive direction from the Divine Spirit.

When your expression is imbalanced, you may at times suppress what you are really feeling. You block input from others by building walls around yourself. This can result in heightened levels of anxiety, secrecy, frustration and anger. Your joyful and creative spirit is damaged and when you finally begin to speak-as you eventually will-it will be in the voice of your wounded inner child. He or she will be angry and will lash out, either outwardly against others or inwardly through destructive or addictive behaviors. Severe imbalances might result in speech or auditory difficulties.

Another common imbalance is refraining from expressing your needs or establishing boundaries because you might offend someone. Learning to speak your mind can be difficult, especially when trying to convey anger. We are often taught that being angry and expressing it is a bad thing. However, remember that there is nothing inappropriate about having feelings and expressing them.

The Collum Chakra, too, can be out of balance in the opposite direction. You can express yourself too much, too recklessly. By using non-stop talking as a means of distancing yourself and avoiding intimate connections with others, you just as effectively drive people from your life.

Trivia holds the power of Nature

Trivia is the form of Hecate that rules the forces of nature in the outer world and giving us their help and guidance, including animals, birds and plants (flowers). She is Hecate as the wild nature Goddess. She is the seductive power of Hecate, the inner allure that takes us within. As such she is another aspect of Hecate operative on the Earth plane through nature.

Yet Trivia has her martial prowess as well. She brings all the forces of nature to help us in our spiritual practice. She is the voice of Hecate as the call of the wild, which is also the call of the unknown and the allure of the inner world. She grants the healing and creative powers of all nature.

Invocation:

While concentrating on the Collum Chakra, chant TRIVIA, allow the buzz of the A "AH" to be felt inside the Chakra.

The Cerebrum Chakra

The Cerebrum Chakra is situated within the Sushumna Nadi and its corresponding center in the physical body is at the space between the two eyebrows. The presiding goddess is Hecate Luna, and the overlord is the Goddess Luna herself. The Chakra is of pure white color or like that of the full moon. This Chakra corresponds to Luna Caelum. The corresponding center in the physical body is at the Cavernous Plexus.

He who concentrates at this center destroys all the Karmas of past lives. The benefits that are derived by meditation on this Chakra cannot be described in words. The practitioner who becomes absorbed in this Chakra is liberated while living. This Chakra has full function over the brain.

Cerebrum Chakra Facts:

- Mental and Emotional Issues:
  Self-evaluation, truth, intellectual abilities,
  feelings of adequacy, openness to ideas of
  others, ability to learn from experiences,
  emotional intelligence, clairvoyance, intuition
  and insight.

- Traits When Overactive:
  Egotism, cynicism, proud, manipulative,
  religiously dogmatic, authoritarian.

- Traits When Under-functioning or Off-balance:
  Difficulty imagining, overly intellectual (only
  able to deal with concrete concepts), overly
  linear or rational thinking. Lack of
  concentration, tension, headaches, eye problems,
  bad dreams, and being overly detached from the
  world.

- Organs: Brain, nervous system, eyes, ears, nose,
  pineal gland, pituitary gland.

- Physical Dysfunctions: Brain
  tumor/hemorrhage/stroke, neurological
  disturbances, blindness/deafness, full spinal
  difficulties, learning disabilities, seizures,

schizophrenia.

- Foods: Lecithin, wheat germ, barley, vitamin E, alfalfa, chamomile, water, water, water.

Hecate Luna holds the power of purification

Hecate Luna is the fierce or fiery form of Hecate. She represents Hecate's fire hidden in the material nature and in the recesses of our bodies and mind. As she awakens, she initiates and propels the upward process of the Inner path in a powerful way. Hecate Luna is the goddess at the root of the world. Hecate Luna is the power of purification!

Hecate Luna's fire can destroy all negative forces, the lower forces that assail us. It is her fire that brings about the deep transmutation at the core of our being. Hecate becomes Hecate Luna to protect, purify and transform us.

Invocation:

While concentrating on the Cerebrum Chakra, chant Luna, allow the buzz of the "OO" and "AH" to be felt inside the Chakra.

The Vertex Chakra

The Vertex Chakra is the abode of Hecate Sol. This corresponds to Sol Caelum. This is situated at the Vertex of the head. When Hydra is united with Sol Caelum, the Mystic enjoys the Supreme Bliss. When Hydra is taken to this center, the Mystic attains the super-conscious state and the Highest Knowledge. He becomes absorbed in the ocean of Light.

This Chakra is the chief of all the Chakras. All the Chakras have their intimate connection with this center. The sound of this Chakra is the primal sound that created creation.

Vertex Chakra Facts:

- Mental and Emotional Issues: Faith, connection to the higher powers; ability to trust life, values, ethics, and courage;

humanitarianism, selflessness, ability to see larger pattern, faith and inspiration, spirituality and devotion.

- Traits When Overactive: Depression, migraine headaches, constant frustration, psychoses, manic-depressive, unable to process energy.

- Traits When Under-functioning or Off-balance: Lack of inspiration, confusion, depression, alienation from The Divine, hesitation to serve, senility, the detriment of the already mentioned above positive qualities and lessons.

- Organs: Muscular system, skeletal system, skin.

- Physical Dysfunctions: Paralysis, genetic disorders, lupus, bone   cancer, multiple sclerosis, amyorophic lateral sclerosis (ALS), chronic fatigue, sensitivity to light and sound.

- Foods: None. (Simply energy)

- Activities to Balance Crown Chakra: Meditation, guided visualizations, visiting peaceful and quiet surroundings.

"O Hecate Sol! Thou art the mind, the sky, the air, the fire, the water, and the earth. Nothing is outside Thee on Thy transformation. Thou hast become light's consecrated queen to alter Thy own blissful conscious Form in the shape of the world."

Hydra, the serpent power or mystic fire, is the primordial energy that lies dormant or sleeping in the Os Sacrum Chakra, the center of the body. It is called the serpentine or annular power on account of serpentine form. It is an electric fiery occult power, the great pristine force which underlies all organic and inorganic matter.

Hydra is the astronomical power in individual bodies. It is not a material force like electricity, magnetism, centripetal or centrifugal force. It is a spiritual astronomical power. In reality it has no form (Hecate Sol is the "Light" aspect of the goddess). The mind has to follow a particular form in the beginning stage. From this gross form, one can easily, understand the subtle formless Hydra. She is the coiled-up, sleeping Divine power that lies dormant in all beings. She has three and a half coils like a serpent with seven heads reflecting the seven Caelums. When it is awakened, it makes a hissing sound like that of a serpent with the sound of a million rattles, and proceeds to the other Chakras!

Hydra is the Goddess of speech and is praised by all that reside in the Caelums. She Herself, when awakened by the Mystic, achieves for him the illumination. It is She who gives liberation. She is the source of all Knowledge and Bliss. She is pure consciousness itself. She is power. She is breath, the Supreme Force, the Mother all. Hecate rides her like the harlot riding the seven headed beast of the apocalypse. She is in control of the seven headed serpent, she is in control of the seven Caelums. It is by this power that the world exists. Creation, preservation and dissolution are in Her. Only by her power the world is kept up. In every kind of practice the Goddess Hydra is the object of worship in some form or the other. It is active. This inactive power is affected by Mystic practices and becomes active. These two functions, inactive and active, are termed 'sleeping' and 'awakening' of the Hydra!

Invocation:

Chant SOL (soul), let the long "O" sound resonate through the Crown Area.

Hecate's wheel, representing the three (outside spokes) worlds as the gross world, subtle world and mental world. The six points in the center as the six physical Caelums and the center dot as Sol Caelum, the return to the absolute.
(4) personal reference

Meditation on Death

Meditation on death and impermanence are regarded as very important in Hecate devotion for two reasons : (1) it is only by recognizing how precious and how short life is that we are most likely to make it meaningful and to live it fully and (2) by understanding the death process and familiarizing ourselves with it, we can remove fear at the time of death and ensure a good rebirth.

(3) Hydra will not be awakened "properly" if the mystic has strong attachments to the body. Because the way in which we live our lives and our state of mind at death directly influence our future lives, the aim or mark of a spiritual practitioner is to have no fear or regrets at the time of death. People who practice to the best of their abilities will die in a state of great bliss. The mediocre practitioner will die happily. Even the initial practitioner will have neither fear nor dread at the time of death. So one should aim at achieving at least the smallest of these results.

There are two common meditations on death in Hecate mysticism. The first looks at the certainty and imminence of death and what will be of benefit at the time of death, in order to motivate us to make the best use of our lives. The second is a simulation or rehearsal of the actual death process, which familiarizes us with death and takes away the fear of the unknown, thus allowing us to die skillfully. In Hecate mysticism, one is also encouraged to go to a cemetery or burial ground to contemplate on death and become familiar with this inevitable event. A practice called the "Cordolium", skull meditation is often employed inside a cemetery.

The first of these meditations is known as the nine-round death meditation, in which we contemplate the three roots, the nine reasonings, and the three convictions, as described below:

A. DEATH IS CERTAIN

1. There is no possible way to escape death.

2. Life has a definite, inflexible limit and each moment brings us closer to the finality of this life. We are dying from the moment we are born.

3. Death comes in a moment and its time is unexpected. All that separates us from the next life is one breath.

Understanding: To practice the spiritual path and ripen our inner potential by cultivating positive mental qualities and abandoning disturbing mental qualities.

B. THE TIME OF DEATH IS UNCERTAIN

4. The duration of our lifespan is uncertain. The young can die before the old, the healthy before the sick, etc.

5. There are many causes and circumstances that lead to death, but few that favor the sustenance of life.

Even things that sustain life can kill us, for example food, motor vehicles, property.

6. The weakness and fragility of one's physical body contribute to life's uncertainty.

The body can be easily destroyed by disease, accident or disasters.

Conviction: To ripen our inner potential now, without delay.

C. THE ONLY THING THAT CAN HELP US AT THE TIME OF DEATH IS OUR MENTAL AND SPIRITUAL DEVELOPMENT

(because all that goes on to the next life is our mind with its karmic, positive or negative, impressions.)

7. Worldly possessions such as wealth, position, money can't help

8. Relatives and friends can neither prevent death nor go with us.

9. Even our own precious body is of no help to us. We have to leave it behind like a shell, an empty husk, an overcoat.

Conviction: To ripen our inner potential purely, without staining our efforts with attachment to worldly concerns.

The second meditation simulates or rehearses the actual death process. Knowledge of this process is particularly important because advanced practitioners can engage in a series of practices that are modeled on death, intermediate state, Caelums and rebirth until they gain such control over them that they are no longer subject to ordinary uncontrolled death and rebirth. This is one of the reasons why Hecate worship is so important.

It is therefore essential for the practitioner to know the stages of death and the mind-body relationship behind them. The description of this is based on a presentation of the winds, or currents of energy, that serve as foundations for various levels of consciousness, and the channels in which they flow. Upon the serial collapse of the ability of these winds to serve as bases of consciousness, the internal and external events of death unfold. Through the power of meditation, the mystic makes the coarse winds dissolve into the very subtle life-bearing wind at the heart. This practice mirrors the process that occurs at death and involves concentration on the psychic channels and the Chakras inside the body.

At the channel-centers there are white and red drops, upon which physical and mental health are based. The white is predominant at the top of the head and the red at the Abdomen. These drops have their origin in a white and red drop at the heart center, and this drop is the size of a small pea and has a white top and red bottom. It is called the indestructible drop, since it lasts until death. The very subtle life-bearing wind dwells inside it and, at death, all winds ultimately dissolve into it, whereupon the clear light vision of death dawns.

The physiology of death revolves around changes in the winds, channels and drops. Psychologically, due to the fact that consciousness of varying grossness and subtlety depend on the winds, like a rider on a horse, their dissolving or loss of ability to serve as bases of consciousness induces radical changes in conscious experience.

Death begins with the sequential dissolution of the winds associated with the four elements (earth, water, fire and air). "Earth" refers to the hard factors of the body such as bone, and the dissolution of the wind associated with it means that that wind is no longer capable of serving as a mount or basis for consciousness. As a consequence of its dissolution, the capacity of the wind associated with "water" (the fluid factors of the body) to act as a mount for consciousness becomes more manifest. The ceasing of this capacity in one element and its greater manifestation in another is called "dissolution" - it is not, therefore, a case of gross earth dissolving into water.

Simultaneously with the dissolution of the earth element, four other factors dissolve, accompanied by external signs (generally visible to others) and an internal sign (the inner experience of the dying person). The same is repeated in serial order for the other three elements, with corresponding external and internal signs.

Upon the inception of the fifth cycle the mind begins to dissolve, in the sense that coarser types cease and subtler minds become manifest. First, conceptuality ceases, dissolving into a mind of white appearance. This subtler mind, to which only a vacuity filled by white light appears, is free from coarse conceptuality. It, in turn, dissolves into a heightened mind of red appearance, which then dissolves into a mind of black appearance. At this point all that appears is a vacuity filled by blackness, during which the person eventually becomes unconscious. In time this is cleared away, leaving a totally clear emptiness (the mind of clear light) free from the white, red and black appearances. This is the final vision of death.

This description of the various internal visions correlates closely with the literature on the near-death experience. People who have had a near-death experience often describe moving from darkness (for example a black tunnel) towards a brilliant, peaceful, loving light. Care must be taken though in such comparisons because the near-death experience is not actual death, that is, the consciousness permanently leaving the body.

Since the outer breath ceased some time before (in the fourth cycle), from this point of view the point of actual death is related not to the cessation of the outer breath but to the appearance of the mind of clear light. A person can remain in this state of lucid vacuity for up to three days, after which (if the body has not been ravaged by illness) the external sign of drops of red or white liquid emerging from the nose and sexual organ occur, indicating the departure of consciousness.

Other signs of the consciousness leaving the body are 1) when all heat has left the area of the heart center (in the center of the chest), 2) the body starts to smell or decompose, 3) a subtle awareness that the consciousness has left and the body has become like 'an empty shell.

When the clear light vision ceases, the consciousness leaves the body and passes through the other seven stages of dissolution (black near-attainment, red increase etc.) in reverse order. As soon as this reverse process begins the person is reborn into an intermediate state between lives, with a subtle body that can go instantly wherever it likes, move through solid objects etc., in its journey to the next place of rebirth.

The intermediate state can last from a moment to seven days, depending on whether or not a suitable birthplace is found. If one is not found the being undergoes a "small death", experiencing the eight signs of death as previously described (but very briefly). He/she then again experiences the eight signs of the reverse process and is reborn in a second intermediate state. This can happen for a total of seven births in the intermediate state (making a total of forty-nine days) during which a place of rebirth must be found.

The "small death" that occurs between intermediate states or just prior to taking rebirth is compared to experiencing the eight signs (from the mirage-like vision to the clear light) when going into deep sleep or when coming out of a dream. Similarly also, when entering a dream or when awakening from sleep the eight signs of the reverse process are experienced.

These states of increasing subtlety during death and of increasing grossness during rebirth are also experienced in fainting and orgasm as well as before and after sleeping and dreaming, although not in complete form. It is this great subtlety and clarity of the mind during the death process that makes it so valuable to use for advanced meditation practices, and why such emphasis is put on it in Hecate mysticism. Advanced mystics will often stay in the clear light meditation for several days after the breathing has stopped, engaging in these advanced meditations, and can achieve liberation at this time.

The view of a Hecate devotee is that each living being has a continuity or stream of consciousness that moves from one life to the next. Each being has had countless previous lives and will continue to be reborn again and again without control unless he/she develops his/her mind to the point where, like the mystics mentioned above, he/she gains control over this process. When the stream of consciousness or mind moves from one life to the next it brings with it the karmic imprints or potentialities from previous lives. Karma literally means "action", and all of the actions of body, speech and mind leave an imprint on the mind-stream. These karmas can be negative, positive or neutral, depending on the action. They can ripen at any time in the future, whenever conditions are suitable. These karmic seeds or imprints are never lost.

At the time of death (clear light stage) the consciousness (very subtle mind) leaves the body and the person takes the body of an intermediate state being. They are in the form that they will take in their next life (some texts say the previous life), but in a subtle rather than a gross form. As mentioned previously, it can take up to forty-nine days to find a suitable place of rebirth. This rebirth is propelled by karma and is uncontrolled. In effect the karma of the intermediate state being matches that of its future parents. The intermediate state being has the illusory appearance of its future parents copulating. It is drawn to this place by the force of attraction to its parent of the opposite sex, and it is this desire that causes the consciousness of the intermediate state being to enter the fertilized ovum. This happens at or near the time of conception and the new life has begun.

One will not necessarily be reborn right away. The Greeks describe six realms of existence that one can travel to, these being the hell realms, the ghost realms, the Elysian Fields and the Caelums for the advanced. One's experience in these situations can range from intense suffering in the Tartarus realms to unimaginable pleasures in the god realms of the Caelums. But all of these levels of existence are regarded as unsatisfactory by the spiritual practitioner because no matter how high one goes within this cyclic existence, one may one day fall down again to the lower realms of existence. So the aim of the spiritual practitioner is to develop his/her mind to the extent where a stop is put to this uncontrolled rebirth, as mentioned previously. The practitioner realizes that all six levels of existence are ultimately in the nature of suffering, so wishes to be free of them forever.

The state of mind at the time of death is regarded as extremely important, because this plays a vital part in the situation one is reborn into. This is one reason why suicide is regarded in mysticism as very unfortunate, because the state of mind of the person who commits suicide is usually depressed and negative and is likely to throw them into a lower rebirth. Also, it doesn't end the suffering, it just postpones it to another life.

When considering the spiritual care of the dying, it can be helpful to divide people into several different categories, because the category they are in will determine the most useful approach to use. These categories are: 1) whether the person is conscious or unconscious, and 2) whether they have a religious belief or not. In terms of the first category, if the person is conscious they can do the practices themselves or someone can assist them, but if they are unconscious someone has to do the practices for them. For the second category, if a person has specific religious beliefs, these can be utilized to help them. If they do not, they still need to be encouraged to have positive/virtuous thoughts at the time of death, such as reminding them of positive things they have done during their life.

For a spiritual practitioner, it is helpful to encourage them to have thoughts such as love, compassion, remembering their spiritual path. It is beneficial also to have an alter in the room or some other spiritual figure that may have meaning for the dying person. It may be helpful for those who are with the dying person to say some prayers, recite Hecate hymns. This could be silent or aloud, whatever seems most appropriate.

However, one needs to be very sensitive to the needs of the dying person. The most important thing is to keep the mind of the person happy and calm. Nothing should be done (including certain spiritual practices) if this causes the person to be annoyed or irritated.

Because the death process is so important, it is best not to disturb the dying person with noise or shows of emotion. Expressing attachment and clinging to the dying person can disturb the mind and therefore the death process, so it is more helpful to mentally let the person go, to encourage them to move on to the next life without fear. It is important not to deny death or to push it away, just to be with the dying person as fully and openly as possible, trying to have an open and deep sharing of the person's fear, pain, joy, love, etc.

As mentioned previously, when a person is dying, their mind becomes much more subtle, and they are more open to receiving mental messages from those people close to them. So silent communication and prayer can be very helpful. It is not necessary to talk much. The dying person can be encouraged to let go into the light, into Hecate's love etc. (again, this can be verbal or mental).

It can be very helpful to encourage the dying person to use breathing meditation - to let go of the thoughts and concentrate on the movement of the breath. This can be helpful for developing calmness, for pain control, for acceptance, for removing fear. It can help the dying person to get in touch with their inner stillness and peace and come to terms with their death. This breathing technique can be especially useful when combined with a mantra, prayer, or affirmation (i.e. half on the in-breath, half on the out-breath).

In Dark Goddess mysticism, it is important to know that for up to about twenty-one days after a person dies they are more connected to the previous life than to the next one. So for this period in particular the loved ones can be encouraged to continue their (silent) communication with the deceased person - to say their good-byes, finish any unfinished business, reassure the dead person, encourage them to let go of their old life and to move on to the next one. It can be reassuring even just to talk to the dead person and at some level to know that they are probably receiving your message. The mind of the deceased person at this stage can still be subtle and receptive.

For the more adept practitioners there is also the method of transference of consciousness at the time of death. With training, at the time of death, the practitioner can project his mind upwards from his heart center through his Vertex directly to one of the Caelums, or at least to a higher rebirth. Someone who has perfected this training can also assist others at the time of death to project their mind to a good rebirth.

It is believed that if the consciousness leaves the body of the dead person through the Vertex or from a higher part of the body, it is likely to result in a good type of rebirth. Conversely, if the consciousness leaves from a lower part of the body this is likely to result in rebirth in one of the lower realms. For this reason, when a person dies it is believed that the first part of the body that should be touched is the Vertex. The Vertex is located about eight finger widths (of the person being measured) back from the (original) hairline. To rub or tap this area or gently pull the Vertex hair after a person dies is regarded as very beneficial and may well help the person to obtain a higher rebirth. There are special sigils of Hecate that can be written on the Vertex after death which also facilitates this process.

Once the consciousness has left the body (which, as mentioned earlier, can take up to three days) it doesn't matter how the body is disposed of or handled (including the carrying out of a post-mortem examination) because in effect it has just become an empty shell. However, if the body is disposed of before the consciousness has left, this will obviously be very disturbing for the person who is going through the final stages of psychological dissolution. When the body expels the liquids as the person drops the body, it is similar to a highly pleasurable orgasm. Hence the word orgasm in Latin means "little death."

Meditation on Tartarus

Meditation on Tartarus serves a very different purpose. One of the essential goals of the adept mystic is to have the endurance or strength to handle the experience of their deity. Merging into the diety is the point of all mystical practice. In this case we are discussing Mother Hecate. In order to experience her in her totality we have to merge into her power. Although Hecate is unique in the fact that she exists in the heaven, earth and Tartarus, it is in the underworld where her true power is alive. When Hecate joins in sexual union with Typhon, she becomes Hecate Aidonaia, Queen of Tartarus. Before we move forward, here is the definition of Tartarus:

In classic mythology, below Heaven, Earth, and Pontus is Tartarus, or Tartaros (Greek Τάρταρος, deep place). It is a deep, gloomy place, a pit, or an abyss used as a dungeon of torment and suffering that resides beneath the underworld. In the Gorgias, Plato (c. 400 BC) wrote that souls were judged after death and those who received punishment were sent to Tartarus. As a place of punishment, it can be considered a hell.

In Greek mythology, Tartarus is both a deity and a place in the underworld even lower than Hades. In ancient Orphic sources and in the mystery schools Tartarus is also the unbounded first-existing entity from which the Light and the cosmos are born.

In Hesiod's Theogony, c. 700 BC, the deity Tartarus was the third force to manifest in the yawning void of Chaos.

As for the place, the Greek poet Hesiod asserts that a bronze anvil falling from heaven would fall 9 days before it reached the Earth. The anvil would take nine more days to fall from Earth to Tartarus. That would make 7625651,04 meters, so the distance between the Heaven to Earth or Earth to Tartarus would also be 7625,65 kilometers. Heaven to Tartarus would be the double: 15.251,8 kilometers. That would be a 3/100 of Moon to Earth distance, though, but much more than the earth atmosphere edge.

In The Iliad (c. 700), Zeus asserts that Tartarus is "as far beneath Hades as heaven is high above the earth." As a place so far from the Sun and so deep in the earth, Tartarus is hemmed in by three layers of night. It is a dank and wretched pit engulfed in murky gloom. It is one of the primordial objects that sprung from Chaos (along with Gaia (Earth) and Eros (Love)).

While, according to Greek mythology, The Realm of

Hades is the place of the dead, Tartarus also has a number of inhabitants. When Cronus, the ruling Titan, came to power he imprisoned the Cyclopes in Tartarus. Some myths also say he imprisoned the three Hecatonchires (giants with fifty heads and one hundred arms). Zeus released them, and defeated Kampe, to aid in his conflict with the Titan giants. The gods of Olympus eventually defeated the Titans. Many, but not all of the Titans, were cast into Tartarus. Epimetheus, Metis, and Prometheus are some Titans who were not banished to Tartarus. Cronus was imprisoned in Tartarus. In Tartarus, the Hecatonchires guarded prisoners. Later, when Zeus overcame the monster Typhon, the offspring of Tartarus and Gaia, he threw the monster into the same pit..

Originally, Tartarus was used only to confine dangers to the gods of Olympus. In later mythologies, Tartarus became the place where the punishment fits the crime. For example Sisyphus, who was punished for telling the father of Aegina, a young woman kidnapped by Zeus for one of his sexual gratifications, where she was and who had initially taken her. Zeus considered this an ultimate betrayal and saw to it that Sisyphus was forced to roll a large boulder up a mountainside, which, when he reached the crest, rolled back down, repeatedly.

Also found there was Ixion, one of the mortals invited to dine with the gods. Ixion began to lust after Zeus' *wife, Hera, and began to caress her under the table, but soon ceased at Zeus' warning. Later that night, having given Ixion a place to sleep, Zeus felt the need to test the guest's tolerance and willpower. Constructing a cloud-woman to mirror Hera in appearance, Zeus sent her, known as Nephele, to Ixion's bed. He promptly slept with and impregnated the false Hera. As his punishment, he was banished to Tartarus to forever roll strapped to a wheel of flames, which represented his burning lust.*

Tantalus who was also graciously invited to dine with the gods, felt he should repay them for their kindness and hospitality, but in his pride, decided to see if he could deceive the gods. Tantalus murdered and roasted his son Pelops as a feast for the gods. Demeter, one of the goddesses who preferred to walk with the mortals, graciously accepted the food, but was immediately repulsed when she bit into the left shoulder. The gods all became violently ill and immediately left for Mt. Olympus. As his punishment for such a heinous act, Tantalus was chained to a rock in the middle of a river in Tartarus with a berry bush hanging just out of reach above his head. Cursed with unquenchable thirst and unending hunger, Tantalus constantly tried to reach the water or food, but each time, the water and berries would recede out of his reach for eternity. It is from Tantalus's name and torment that we derive the English word "tantalise."

According to Plato (c. 400), Rhadamanthus, Aeacus and Minos were the judges of the dead and chose who went to Tartarus. Rhadamanthus judged Asian souls; Aeacus judged European souls and Minos was the deciding vote and judge of the Greek.

Through years of single pointed devotion to Hecate, she will start to move you into the underworld. This can also be enhanced by choosing to worship her in one of her CHTHONIC forms. Hecate Aidonaia, Chthonia, Antaia or Prytania is sufficient. The first and foremost feeling is *terror*. I have several clients that mentioned complete fear of sitting in their alter when this process starts. It is not just the fear of dying it is the feeling of suffering that comes forth from Tartarus. After sitting in this feeling, you start to build a strength that is unshakable by worldly circumstances. One of the great advantages of worshiping Hecate is endurance. A real Hecate devotee can endure anything. Meditating on the power of Hecate, in one of her Chthonic forms, prepares you for death and gives you unshakable endurance.

After a prolonged period of worshiping Hecate in one of her underworld forms, spiritual experiences follow. Dreams, omens, visions and divine communication with Hecate commences. In Greek and Hindu mysticism it takes 7 years of focusing on one deity to start having divine experiences, 14 years for divine communication and 21 years to develop the powers of the deity. This is why single pointed devotion to a deity is so important.

If you want peace, you have to overcome fear. Fear creates weakness and a lack inner strength.

The great master Ramakrishna said that if you can experience God in the lowest you can experience God in everything. Tartarus represents one of the most difficult energies in the universe, one who is unaffected by the suffering of Tartarus, is completely unaffected by negative energy, hence peace prevails.

Hecate, Goddess of Supreme Consciousness

In Dark Goddess mysticism, Hecate is the first of the Great Astronomical Powers, because in a certain way she is the one who "spins the wheel of the universal time."

On the other hand, at the end of the manifested world, she devours all the universes and the three planes of creation: the physical, the astral and the causal universes.

The "Great Astronomical Power" Hecate finally devours the time itself and this is the very reason why Hecate is viewed as the primordial cause of creation and destruction of the universe.

Hecate is the everything, representing both the being (the existence) and the infinite consciousness in manifestation.

According to the Chaldean belief, the whole manifested world springs from the Infinite Consciousness of the illumined union between light (inactive state) and Hecate (the active state).

The knowledge of creation bears the name Hecate. The universe thus created has to be maintained in the manifestation, function performed by Hecate.

Nonetheless, both the creation and the preserving aspects imply a molecular "death" or "destruction" of each form of the universe, function performed by Hecate.

Her darkness dissolves everything

The simultaneous existence of these three processes within the creation clearly expresses the statements included in all ancient Greek writings, that the creation of the universe did not occur once, in the past, nor will the universe be destroyed once in the future, and that rather in every instant these aspects manifest as rays creating the illusion of continuity and reality.

Although the human body and mind are permanently assailed by innumerable sensorial perceptions, the state of divine ecstasy implies the disappearance of all mental functions and of the physical awareness into the Supreme consciousness of Sol Caelum, that which is beyond all duality.

From a different perspective, Hecate is also the creator of universes, as they come to life from the ashes of the "Divine Consciousness" and the purifying fire of this Black Goddess. Consequently, Hecate's action is deeply evolutionary, as she impels the human beings towards evolution, sometimes in a challenging manner.

Nonetheless, Hecate performs her actions in divine

light and harmony, knowing that this is the best thing to do. Those who manage to pass all the tests and go through all the stages are in truth spiritual warriors, and they will be rewarded with Hecate's spiritual grace.

Hecate is the time beyond time

Hecate has been associated and often equated with Nyx (night), the first of the Great Astronomical Powers.

Hecate is also named Nyctipolus, in her quality of energy and terrible Cosmic Power who impels humankind towards action and the universe towards manifestation.

Hecate's representation reveals her holding a torch. This is not a trivial manner of representing a fire, but instead this fact stands for the transcendence of all limitations, the holder of light.

Her action in the manifested world implies the destroying and in the same time purifying action of time.

However, as the mystic is more and more concerned with spiritual aspects, and firmly oriented towards obtaining spiritual freedom at all costs, he or she will be blessed with Hecate's overwhelming grace.

She destroys the ego

One of the most important hypo-stasis in which one can worship Hecate, is the one who defeated the Giant Clytius. This Giant represents the forces of ignorance in Greek spirituality.

For the worshiper of God in the aspect of the Divine Mother, Hecate is the only hypostasis that destroys the evil of the world in its numerous aspects.

Thus, Greek mythology describes how the goddess has vanquished the Giant Clytius, saving the gods from captivity and who set up the divine order in the universe.

Hecate grants her support and help to those who ask for it and worship her, so that the spiritual forces develop and gain supremacy over the negative influences of the psychic and mental.

Hecate is thus the "Divine Light" who destroys and burns in the terrible fire of her pure consciousness, any malefic force and leftover ignorance.

Her force awakens Hydra

The spiritual practice recommended for the worship of the Great Hecate implies the effort of purifying and activating the Chakras, so that the fundamental energy Hydra ascends from Saturnus Caelum to Sol Caelum.

The ascension of Hydra represents one of the most important aspects of this Great Astronomical Goddess.

The mysterious influence of Hecate is so complex and hidden that only few pure souls may see through her actions their real significance. Hence she is Trivia, the Great Mystery.

We meet a frequent representation of Hecate as the Cosmic Mother, surrounded by a great number of different gods and goddesses. Lacking any dimensions or spatial-temporal limits, she takes on different forms and names in order to meet her worshiper's most secret desires.

In certain situations, Hecate embarks into action to destroy that which is weak, or useless. Thus, we may see her representation as having six arms, in which she holds different objects that are helpful in restoring or preserving the divine order of the universe.

In her most elevated aspect, Hecate Soteira is the Divine Bliss itself, that which is beyond ordinary human perception, and the nature of conscious Light.

Consequently, there are two ways of worshiping her: as the great Goddess bestowing her grace and blessings upon all those who deserve it, and as holy energy who grants spiritual freedom (Sol Caelum).

The purifying fire that burns the ego to ashes

Hecate is black, the source of all colors. This also indicates the fact that she is associated with the depths of God's mystery.

However, this terrible and scaring aspect is backed up by a smiling attitude of the goddess, looking upon the being of the universe with kindness and affection, sustaining their life and nourishing them with her three heads.

Her ironic laughter is for all those who, due to ignorance, imagine that they can elude spiritual evolution. The Great Goddess has three all-seeing heads, "supervising" the universes from the past, present and future. No one can escape her glance!

As Hecate Sol, she holds a skull on the left and a whip on the right, whose significance is double: on one hand it is the receiver of the universal mysterious teaching (whip representing task), and on the other hand it is a reminder of what endures after the dissolution of the body (bones).

Through her infinite grace, all universe dissolves in her

Hecate holds an athame, whose role is to cut all worldly connections and attachments, so that the worshiper is prepared for the ultimate spiritual freedom.

It is also interesting to mention that her hair is long and disheveled, representing the power of Hecate's all-pervading grace.

Her benevolence and compassion are underlined by two of her hands, one holding a torch, representing casting away fear and the other hand holding a key, offering spiritual gifts and powers to those that open hidden doors.

Around her neck there is a necklace made of male testicles belonging to various malefic entities, symbolizing her complete victory over the senses.

Her body is splashed with the blood of Clytius, and her earrings are in fact two decapitated human heads. This is Hecate's complex representation in her terrible form, known also as CHTHONIA.

In the Greek iconography, Hecate appears under a number of other forms, with minor differences as regards the number of the arms, face, of symbolic objects she holds.

Thus, Lucifera, Inferna, Trivia, Triceps, Sol, Enodia represent just as many aspects of the Goddess, worshiped in different areas of the Mediterranean.

Among these forms, remarkable is the form of Hecate Soteira, described as a master power, ready to devour any illusory aspect of the universe.

The Practice

(Merging into the Deity)

Hymns and Sigils: As in all spiritual practices, hymns (invocation) play an important part in mystical experience, not only for focusing the mind, often through the conduit of specific gods like Bacchus, Hades and in this case Mother Hecate. Similarly, worship will often involve concentrating on a statue or talisman.

Identification with deities: Paganism, being a development of ancient thought, embraced the gods and goddesses, along the mystical philosophy that each represents an aspect of the absolute. These deities may be worshiped externally (with flowers, incense etc.) but, more importantly, are used as objects of meditation, where the practitioner experiences the 'vision' of the deity of choice. Once the God or Goddess is activated inside the individual, the deity awakens and takes on the form of Hydra who sits in the Os Sacrum Chakra. At this point the deity takes on the personality of a guru and through devotion starts to awaken the other Chakras. There are seven main Caelums and innumerable lesser Caelums (inner worlds) inside the main Caelums. The Caelums exist inside the Chakras. *(refer to the book Hecate I: Death, Transition and Spiritual Mastery for more on this subject)*

. Os Sacrum Chakra (Saturnus Caelum)
. Genitalia Chakra (Jove Caelum)
. Abdomen Chakra (Mavors Caelum)
. Cor Chakra (Venus Caelum)
. Collum Chakra (Mecurius Caelum)
. Cerebrum Chakra (Luna Caleum)
. Vertex Chakra (Sol Caelum)

Concentration on the body: Mystics generally see the body as a microcosm; for example, the practitioner meditates on the Cerebrum as the moon, the heart as Venus and the Genitalia Chakra as the bliss of Jove. Mystics teach that the body contains a series of energy centers (Chakra - "wheel"), which may be associated with elements, planets or occult powers. The phenomenon of Hydra (Kundalini), a flow of energy through the Chakras, is controversial; some teachers see it as essential to realization, while others regard it as unimportant or as an abreaction. As it is, awakening Hydra (Kundalini) is nothing but the flow of the subtle evergy, a spiritual current, that, when moving, opens Chakras and the Caelums inside the Chakras.

The five unacceptables: In the "Left Handed Path of Hecate", the five unacceptables are ritually broken in order to free the practitioner from binding convention. In other words, to remove the "pride" of holiness. Holiness creates separation and later turns to judgment. The five unacceptables are allowed in moderation.

* sex
* wine
* money
* meat
* cannabis

All these unacceptables can assist the mystic spiritually if done without indulgence. Indulgence of any kind disrupts spiritual realization *(social cannabis use is forbidden and should only be used for medical issues and meditation)*.

Hecate's Magical Herbs

The yew, black poplar, cannabis, belladonna and willow are all sacred to Hecate. The leaves of the black poplar are dark on one side and light on the other, symbolizing the boundary between the worlds. The yew has long been associated with the Underworld. The yew has strong associations with death as well as rebirth. A poison prepared from the seeds was used on arrows, and yew wood was commonly used to make bows and dagger hilts. The potion in Hecate's cauldron contains 'slips of yew'. Yew berries carry Hecate's power, and can bring wisdom or death. The seeds are highly poisonous, but the fleshy, coral-colored 'berry' surrounding it is not. If prepared correctly, the berry can cause visual hallucinations. Many other herbs and plants are associated with the Goddess, including garlic, almonds, lavender, thyme, myrrh, mugwort, cardamon, mint, dandelion, hellebore, and lesser celandine. Several poisons and hallucinogens are linked to Hecate, including hemlock, mandrake, aconite, and opium poppy. Many of Hecate's plants were those that can be used shamanistically to achieve varyings states of consciousness.

Deadly Nightshade

Solanum Lethale.
Dwale, or deadly Nightshade.

Atropa belladonna. Common Names: Deadly Nightshade, Dwale, Death's Herb, Witch's Berry

Atropa belladonna is a perennial branching herb growing to 5 feet tall, with 8 inch long ovate leaves. The leaves in first-year Atropa belladonna plants are larger than those of older plants. The flowers are bell-shaped, blue-purple or dull red, followed by a shiny, black or purple 0.5 inch berry.

Atropa Belladonna (Deadly Nightshade, Witches

Berry) was used in witchcraft, being equated with aggressive female sexuality and feelings of flight. It has been suggested that the ointment made from the plant may have been inserted into the vagina with an anointed broom or staff, where it was absorbed by the body, thus accounting for the common image of witches flying on brooms. The active chemical, Atropine, is used in medicinal drugs today.

In earlier times in Italy, women used extracts of Atropa belladonna to dialate their eyes for cosmetic purposes; such use explains the origin of the common name (Italian, "beautiful woman"). Belladonna was also an important ingredient in Witches brew during the Middle ages, often being equated with sexuality. A flying ointment salve was made from this plant along with others, and rubbed on the bodies of women. Experiments have shown that the subjective sensation of flight was a common theme with subjects under the influence of solanaceous compounds, not unlike what was reportedly experienced by witches.

Description

The plant has dull green leaves. The flowers are bell-shaped and are a dull, unremarkable shade of purple, which yield shiny black berries about 1 cm in diameter. It is a herbaceous shrub, and can grow to be about one metre tall. The leaves have an unctuous, "poison ivy"-like feel to them; they can indeed cause vesicular pustular eruptions if handled carelessly.

Many animals, such as rabbits, birds and deer, seem to eat the plant with impunity, not suffering any deleterious effects, though dogs and cats are affected. Many reports suggest that some humans have been poisoned simply by eating animals that have eaten some of the leaves, although these reports may be possibly apocryphal.

Germination is often difficult due to the presence of germination inhibitors in the seeds. Because of its name, it is not common as a garden plant, and is considered a weed in some places. It is not as hardy a perennial as the literature would lead one to believe, and will not tolerate transplantation. Germination requires several weeks in warm, moist, absolutely sterile soil, usually far from normal garden conditions.

Toxicity

Berries of the *belladonna*

True to its name, it is one of the most toxic plants to be found in the Western hemisphere. Children have been poisoned by as few as three of the berries, and a small leaf thoroughly chewed can be a fatal dose for an adult. The root is often the most toxic part, though this can vary from one specimen to another.

All parts of the plant, especially the berries, contain the extremely toxic alkaloid atropine. The approximate lethal dose for an adult is three berries, although fewer can be fatal. Symptoms of belladonna poisoning are the same as those for atropine, and include dilated pupils, tachycardia, hallucinations, blurred vision, loss of balance, a feeling of flight, staggering, a sense of suffocation, paleness followed by a red rash, flushing, husky voice, extremely dry throat, constipation, urinary retention, and confusion. The skin can completely dry out and slough off. Fatal cases have a rapid pulse that turns feeble. The antidote is the same as for atropine.

The plant is also toxic to animals; for instance, poisoning can lead to colic, depression, weakness, and lack of coordination in horses, with fatalities reported even for small amounts from 1–10 lbs.

Cosmetics

The name *belladonna* originates from the historic use by *Bella Donnas* (Italian for *beautiful ladies*) to dilate their pupils; an extract of belladonna was used as eye drops as part of their makeup preparations. The atropine content of the fluid had the effect of dilating the pupil, thus making their eyes supposedly more attractive. Dilated pupils are considered more attractive (especially with females) because pupils normally dilate when a person is aroused, thus making eye contact much more intense than it already is. It had the side effect of making their vision a little blurry and making their heart rates increase.

Witchcraft

According to practitioners of witchcraft, nightshade is ruled by Hecate and can turn into an old hag on Walpurgis Night, or April 30. It is also used in flying ointments. Of the twelve recipes for flying ointments, six call for deadly nightshade.

According to legend, this is the favorite plant of the devil, and can only be harmed when he is diverted from its care on the Walpurgis.

Modern medicine

The plant is the most important source of atropine, ironically an effective cure for the effects of poisoning by potent cholinesterase inhibitors such as Parathion, Malathion and, most infamously, Sarin, VX, and similar nerve agents. In Europe, it is specifically cultivated for that reason.

Optometrists and ophthamologists use belladonna to this day for pupil dilation in eye examinations, though the dose is extremely small.

Recreational drug

Occasionally, the plant is used for recreational purposes: it is consumed in the form of either a tea or simply raw, which can produce vivid hallucinations, described by many as a 'living dream'. The effects of even a slight poisoning are so unpleasant that the recreational user is unlikely to attempt its use again, if he or she survives at all.

Cannabis κάνναβις (kánnabis)

"The original purpose of cannabis was to remove the veil of this world to enter the next. What ever actions you take to help you remove this veil is permitted, there is no negative karma in the attempt to realize the self. When cannabis is used for any other purpose it creates the opposite affect of bad karma which creates a greater veil of ignorance and fuels the shadow self. Cannabis should ONLY be used to pierce the veil! Only the intelligent should consider the use of Cannabis spiritually."- Jade Sol Luna

In Greece, Hecate was often called Enodia, who, in
turn, was a goddess of witchcraft, drugs and
Cannabis in Thessaly (Johnston 24)

Cannabis has been apart of the Goddess in the
Mediterranean since the Etruscan time and was first
removed by those who sought to eliminate the
Goddess from Religion. In most ancient hunter-
gatherer societies in Rome, women balanced the
males' hunting mentality with their shamanistic plants
from the surrounding wilderness. Women therefore
became the first to learn the secrets of plants and the
mystical side of nature.

Cannabis is among humanity's oldest and most useful
cultivated crops, and so it is not surprising to find that
cannabis, in all its forms, has been intricately
associated with Goddess worship in many cultures,
throughout history.

Hecate and Cannabis

One of the most ancient goddesses in the
Mediterranean still worshiped in the world today is
the Mother Hecate, the Goddess of life and death.
Hecate is generally depicted with three heads, and
represents the dark aspect of the goddess trinity of
virgin-mother-crone. Both ancient and modern
devotees of Hecate partake of cannabis in various
forms as a part of their worship.

Devotional ceremonies to Hecate involve cannabis ingestion, which is directed at raising the power of Hydra from the base of the spine through the Chakras.

Hecate is the Greek counterpart of the ferocious and sensual Canaanite goddess Anath, (part of a similar trinity with Ashera and Astarte) who is also described with "attached heads to her back, girded hands to her waist."

In ancient Germany, cannabis was used in association with Freya, the slightly tamer Hecate-like goddess of Love and Death.

In Scythian myth, Rhea Krona came to reap her children in death with the scythe, an agricultural tool named for its Scythian origin, and originally designed for harvesting cannabis. This scythe image has survived through patriarchal times and into our modern day, with both Saturn and the Grim Reaper still carrying Rhea Krona's ancient hemp-harvesting tool.

Ancient shamanic use

Several of the mummies found near Turpan in Xinjiang province of Northwestern China were buried with sacks of cannabis next to them. Based on this, archaeologists concluded that they were shamans: "The cannabis must have been buried with the dead shamans who dreamed of continuing the profession in another world." The mummies were dated to circa 1,000 BCE.

The early Chinese pharmacopeia Shen Nong Ben Cao Jing referred to magical uses of cannabis such as seeing demons and communicating with spirits. Early Taoists also believed that combining cannabis with ginseng allowed one to see into the future. A 6th-century CE Taoist medical work, Wu Zang Jing, recommended cannabis for seeing demons or spirits, and in this Joseph Needham found evidence for the influence of cannabis in the communications with immortals recorded by a Taoist named Yangxi in the 4th century.

Herodotus wrote: "The Scythians, as I said, take some of this hemp-seed, and, creeping under the felt coverings, throw it upon the red-hot stones; immediately it smokes, and gives out such a vapour as no Grecian vapour-bath can exceed; the Scyths, delighted, shout for joy." What Herodotus called the "hemp-seed" must have been the whole flowering tops of the plant, where the psychoactive resin is produced along with the fruit ("seeds")

Ancient Pagan use

In ancient Germanic culture, cannabis was associated with the Norse love goddess, Freya. The harvesting of the plant was connected with an erotic high festival. It was believed that Freya lived as a fertile force in the plant's feminine flowers and by ingesting them one became influenced by this divine force. The Celts may have also used cannabis, as evidence of hashish traces were found in Hallstatt, birthplace of Celtic culture. In Greece, Hecate was known as the Goddess of sacred herbs and cannabis was an instrument in experiencing her.

Hindu and Buddhist use

Cannabis was used in Hindu culture as early as 1500 BCE, and its ancient use is confirmed within the Vedas (Sama Veda, Rig Veda, and Atharva Veda).

Cannabis or ganja is associated with worship of the Hindu god Shiva, who is popularly believed to like the hemp plant. Ganja is offered to Shiva images, especially on Shivratri festival. This practice is particularly witnessed at temples of Benares, Baidynath and Tarakeswar.

Ganja is not only offered to the god, but also consumed by Shaivite (sect of Shiva) yogis. Charas is smoked by some Shaivite devotees and cannabis itself is seen as a gift ("prasad," or offering) to Shiva to aid in sadhana. Some of the wandering ascetics in India known as sadhus smoke charas out of a clay chillum.

During the Hindu festival of Holi, people consume a drink called bhang which contains cannabis flowers. According to one description, when elixir of life was produced from the churning of the ocean by the gods and the demons, Shiva created cannabis from his own body to purify the elixir (whence, for cannabis, the epithet angaj or body-born). Another account suggests that the cannabis plant sprang when a drop of the elixir dropped on the ground. Thus, cannabis is used by sages due to association with elixir and Shiva. Wise drinking of bhang, according to religious rites, is believed to cleanse sins, unite one with Shiva and avoid the miseries of hell in the after-life. In contrast, foolish drinking of bhang without rites is considered a sin.

Researchers claim that in the 5th century BCE Siddhartha ate only hemp seeds for six years, prior to becoming the Buddha. Cannabis continues to play a significant role in the meditation ritual of Tibetan Tantric Buddhism, and has been a practice since 500 BCE when cannabis was regarded as a holy plant.

Ancient Hebraic use

According to Aryeh Kaplan, cannabis was an ingredient in the Holy anointing oil mentioned in various sacred Hebrew texts. The herb of interest is most commonly known as kaneh-bosem (קְנֵה- בֹ שֶׂ)is mentioned several times in the Old Testament as a bartering material, incense, and an ingredient in Holy anointing oil used by the high priest of the temple.

The Septuagint (300 BCE) translates kaneh-bosem as

calamus, and this translation has been propagated unchanged to most later translations of the Torah (1500 BCE+). However, Polish anthropologist Sula Benet published etymological arguments that the Aramaic word for hemp can be read as kannabos and appears to be a cognate to the modern word 'cannabis',with the root kan meaning reed or hemp and bosm meaning fragrant. Both cannabis and calamus are fragrant, reed-like plants containing psychotropic compounds. While Benet's conclusion regarding the psychoactive use of cannabis is not universally accepted among Jewish scholars, there is general agreement that cannabis is used in talmudic sources to refer to hemp fibers, as hemp was a vital commodity before linen replaced it.

Muslim use

In Islam, the use of cannabis is deemed to be khamr (intoxicant), and therefore haraam (forbidden).

Although cannabis use in some societies in Islamic countries has been present, often but not exclusively in the lower classes, its use explicitly for spiritual purposes is most noted among the Sufi. According to one Arab legend, Haydar, the Persian founder of the religious order of Sufi, came across the cannabis plant while wandering in the Persian mountains. Usually a reserved and silent man, when he returned to his monastery after eating some cannabis leaves, his disciples were amazed at how talkative and animated (full of spirit) he seemed. After cajoling Haydar into telling them what he had done to make him feel so happy, his disciples went out into the mountains and tried the cannabis for themselves. So it was, according to the legend, the Sufis came to know the pleasures of hashish.

Sikh use

The Sikh religion developed in the Punjab in Mughal times. The common use of bhang in religious festivals by Hindus carried over into Sikh practice as well. Sikhs were required to observe Dasehra with bhang, in commemoration of the founder of the Sikh religion, Guru Nanak.

The Indian Hemp Drugs Commission Report describes the traditional use of cannabis in the Sikh religion.

Among the Sikhs the use of bhang as a beverage appears to be common, and to be associated with their religious practices. The witnesses who refer to this use by the Sikhs appear to regard it as an essential part of their religious rites having the authority of the Granth or Sikh scripture. Witness Sodhi Iswar Singh, Extra Assistant Commissioner, says :"As far as I know, bhang is pounded by the Sikhs on the Dasehra day, and it is ordinarily binding upon every Sikh to drink it as a sacred draught by mixing water with it. Legend--Guru Gobind Singh, the tenth guru, the founder of the Sikh religion, was on the gaddi of Baba Nanak in the time of Emperor Aurangzeb. When the guru was at Anandpur, tahsil Una, Hoshiarpur district, engaged in battle with the Hill Rajas of the Simla, Kangra, and the Hoshiarpur districts, the Rains sent an elephant, who was trained in attacking and slaying the forces of the enemy with a sword in his trunk and in breaking open the gates of forts, to attack and capture the Lohgarh fort near Anandpur. The guru gave one of his followers, Bachittar Singh, some bhang and a little of opium to eat, and directed him to face the said elephant. This brave man obeyed the word of command of his leader and attacked the elephant, who was intoxicated and had achieved victories in several battles before, with the result that the animal was overpowered and the Hill Rajas defeated. The use of bhang, therefore, on the Dasehra day is necessary as a sacred draught. It is customary among the Sikhs generally to drink bhang, so that Guru Gobind Singh has himself is said to have said the following poems in praise of bhang: "Give me, O Saki (butler), a cup of green color (bhang), as it is required by me at the time of battle . "Bhang is also used on the Chandas day, which is a festival of the god Sheoji Mahadeva. The Sikhs consider it binding to use it on the Dasehra day-The quantity then taken is too small to prove injurious." As Sikhs are absolutely prohibited by their religion from smoking, the use of ganja and charas in this form is not practiced by them. of old Sikh times, is annually permitted to collect without interference a boat load of bhang, which is afterwards. distributed throughout the year to the sadhus and beggars who are supported by the dharamsala.

Rastafari use

Members of the Rastafari movement use cannabis as a part of their worshiping of God, Bible study and Meditation. The movement was founded in Jamaica in the 1930s and while it is not known when Rastafarians first made cannabis into something sacred it is clear that by the late 1940s Rastafari was associated with cannabis smoking at the Pinnacle community of Leonard Howell. Rastafari see cannabis as a sacramental and deeply beneficial plant that is the Tree of Life mentioned in the Bible. Bob Marley, amongst many others, said, "the herb ganja is the healing of the nations." The use of cannabis, and particularly of large pipes called chalices, is an integral part of what Rastafari call "reasoning sessions" where members join together to discuss life according to the Rasta perspective. They see cannabis as having the capacity to allow the user to penetrate the truth of how things are much more clearly, as if the wool had been pulled from one's eyes. Thus the Rastafari come together to smoke cannabis in order to discuss the truth with each other, reasoning it all out little by little through many sessions. They see the use of this plant as bringing them closer to nature. In these ways Rastafari believe that cannabis brings the user closer to Jah, Haile Selassie I, and pipes of cannabis are always dedicated to His Imperial Majesty before being smoked. While it is not necessary to use cannabis to be a Rastafari, some feel that they must use it regularly as a part of their faith. "The herb is the key to new understanding of the self, the universe, and God. It is the vehicle to astronomical consciousness" according to Rastafari philosophy, and is believed to burn the corruption out of the human heart. Rubbing the ashes from smoked cannabis is also considered a healthy practice.

Black Popular

Magical History and Associations

In Gaelic tongue the tree was called Peble and Pophuil in the celtic way. Poplar is generally a plant of Jupiter, Saturn and the Sun and is associated with the element of water. Its color is rufous (red) and the bird associated with Poplar is the Whistling Swan. The stones associated with Poplar are Amber, Citrine Quartz, Sapphire and Swan Fluorite. The Anglo-Saxon rune poem seems to refer to the Poplar as being associated with the rune "berkano." Heracles wore a crown of Poplar leaves in triumph after killing the giant Cacus (the evil one) and retrieving Cerberus from Hades. The upper surface of the Poplar leaves was thus darkened from Hades' smokey fumes. Poplar trees are sacred to the Mesopotamian goddess Ua-Ildak. The Grass King of Grossvargula, who was seen as having fertilizing powers, went on horseback wearing a pyramid of Poplar branches and a crown. He led a procession of young men about the town and was then stripped of his branches beneath the Silver Lindens of Sommerberg. Poplar (Aspen) is said to be the tree of the Autumn Equinox and of old age, and is known as the shield makers' tree. The Black Poplar was a funeral tree sacred to Hecate as death goddess, to Egeria, and to Mother Earth. Plato makes a reference to the use of Black Poplar and Silver Fir as an aid in divination. The Silver Fir standing for hope assured and the Black Poplar for loss of hope. The Grove of Persephone in the Far West contained Black Poplars and old Willows. In ancient Ireland, the coffin makers measuring rod was made of Aspen, apparently to remind the dead that this was not the end. In Christian lore, the quaking Poplar (Aspen) was used to construct Christ's cross, and the leaves of the tree quiver when they remember this fact.

Magickal usage

The Poplar's ability to resist and to shield, its association with speech, language and the Winds indicates an ability to endure and conquer. The Poplar is known as the "Tree that Transcends Fear." Poplars symbolize the magick of joy, the aging of the year, resurrection and hope and are connected to the otherworld. Poplar can be used in magick done for success, passage and transformation, hope, rebirth, divinations, shielding, endurance, agility in speech and language, protection, and love - and as an aid in astral projection. Balm of Gilead buds can be carried in tiny red bags to help mend a broken heart. These buds should be kept as close to the heart as possible. Balm of Gilead buds can also be placed under the pillow and slept on to heal a broken heart. It may take several days to feel relief, but this really works. Balm of Gilead is also effective for grief, homesickness and the blues. Poplar can be used in protection charms of all kinds. Poplar is a good wood to burn in balefires and ritual fires since it offers protection. Shields can be made of Poplar since the wood is thought to offer protection from injury or death. Add some Balm of Gilead resin to your tinctures to enhance the "fixing" of the scent and to offer some added protection to the tincture. Carrying Poplar helps to overcome the urge to give way under the burden of worldly pressures, and aids in determination. Poplar buds can also be carried to attract money and can be burned as an incense to create financial security. Siberian reindeer-hunting cultures carved small goddess statues of Poplar (Aspen) wood. Groats and fat were then offered to the figures with prayer.

The Oracle of Pythia and Hallucinogenics

According to earlier myths, the office of the oracle was initially held by the goddesses Themis and Phoebe, and that the site was sacred first to Gaia. Subsequently it was held sacred to Poseidon, the "Earth-shaker" god of earthquakes, and the "Goddess of Witches" Hecate. During the Greek Dark Age, from the 11th to the 9th century BC, the arrival of a new god of prophecy saw the temple being seized by Apollo who expelled the twin guardian serpents of Gaia. Later myths stated that Phoebe or Themis had "given" the site to Apollo, rationalizing its seizure by priests of the new god, but presumably, having to retain the priestesses of the original oracle because of the long tradition. Apparently Poseidon was mollified by the gift of a new site in Troizen.

Diodorus also explained how initially, the Pythia was a young virgin, but one consultant notes, "Echecrates the Thessalian, having arrived at the shrine and beheld the virgin who uttered the oracle, became enamoured of her because of her beauty, carried her away and violated her; and the Delphians because of this deplorable occurrence passed a law that in the future a virgin could no longer prophesy, but that an elderly woman ... would declare the oracles and she would be dressed in the costume of a virgin as a sort of reminder of the prophetess of olden times."

The scholar Martin Litchfield West writes that the Pythia shows many traits of shamanistic practices, likely inherited or influenced from Central Asian practices, although there is no evidence of any Central Asian connection at this time. He cites the Pythia sitting in a cauldron on a tripod, while making her prophecies in an ecstatic trance state, like shamans, and her unintelligible utterings.

The Pythia was probably selected, at the death of her predecessor, from amongst a guild of priestesses of the temple, and was required to be a woman of good character. Although some were married, upon assuming their role as the Pythia, the priestesses ceased all family responsibilities, and individual identity. In the heyday of the oracle, the Pythia may have been a woman chosen from a prominent family, well educated in geography, politics, history, philosophy, and the arts. In later periods, however, uneducated peasant women were chosen for the role, which may explain why the poetic pentameter or hexameter prophecies of the early period, later were made only in prose. The archaeologist John Hale reports:

"The Pythia was (on occasion) a noble woman of aristocratic family, sometimes a peasant, sometimes rich, sometimes poor, sometimes old, sometimes young, sometimes a very lettered and educated woman to whom somebody like the high priest and the philosopher Plutarch would dedicate essays, other times one who could not write her own name. So it seems to have been aptitude rather than any ascribed status that made these women eligible to be Pythias and speak for the God."

During the height of the oracle's popularity, as many as three women served as Pythia, another vestige of the triad, with two taking turns in giving prophecy and another kept in reserve.

Several other officials served the oracle in addition to the Pythia. After 200 BC at any given time there were two priests of Apollo, who were in charge of the entire sanctuary; Plutarch, who served as a priest in the late first century and early second century AD, gives us the most information about the organization of the oracle at that time. Before 200 BC, while the temple was dedicated to Apollo, there was probably only one priest of Apollo. Priests were chosen from among the leading citizens of Delphi, and were appointed for life. In addition to overseeing the oracle, priests would also conduct sacrifices at other festivals of Apollo, and had charge of the Pythian games. Earlier arrangements, before the temple became dedicated to Apollo, are not documented.

The other officials associated with the oracle are less well understood. These are the hosioi ("holy ones") and the prophētai (singular prophētēs). Prophētēs is the origin of the English word "prophet", but a better translation of the Greek word might be "one who speaks on behalf of another person. "The prophetai are referred to in literary sources, but their function is unclear; it has been suggested that they interpreted the Pythia's prophecies, or even reshaped her utterances into verse, but it has also been argued that the term prophētēs is a generic reference to any cult officials at the sanctuary, including the Pythia. There were five hosioi, whose responsibilities are unclear, but may have been involved in some way with the operation of the oracle.

In the traditions associated with Apollo, the oracle gave prophecies only between spring and autumn. In the winter months, Apollo was said to have deserted his temple, his place being taken by his divine half-brother Dionysus, whose tomb was within the temple. It is not known whether the Oracle participated in the

Dionysian rites of the Maenads or Pluto in the Korykion cave on Mount Parnassos, although Plutarch informs us that his friend Clea, was both a Priestess to Apollo and to the secret rites of Dionysus. The male priests seem to have had their own ceremonies to the dying and resurrecting God. Apollo was said to return at the beginning of Spring, on the 7th day of the month of Bysios, his birthday. This also would reiterate the absences of the great goddess Demeter in winter also, which would have been a part of the earliest traditions.

Once a month thereafter the oracle would undergo special rites, including fasting, to prepare Pythia for the event, on the seventh day of the month, sacred to Apollo. Washing in the Castalian Spring, she then received inspiration by drinking of the waters of the Kassotis from the naiad said to be living in the stream that ran beneath the adyton (a Greek word meaning "do not enter") of the temple where she sat.

Descending into her chamber, she mounted her tripod seat, holding laurel leaves and a cauldron of the Kassotis water into which she gazed. Nearby was the omphalos, the navel of Earth, flanked by the two golden eagles of Zeus, and the cleft from which emerged the sacred Pneuma.

Consultants, carrying laurel branches sacred to Apollo approached the temple along the winding upward course of the Sacred Way, bringing a black ram for sacrifice in the forecourt of the temple, and a gift of money for the oracle. Petitioners drew lots to determine the order of admission, but big donations to Apollo could secure them a higher place in line. The ram was first showered with water and observed to ensure that it shivered from the hooves upward, an auspicious sign that the oracular reading could proceed. Upon sacrifice, the animal's organs, particularly its liver, were examined to ensure the signs were favorable.

Between 535 and 615 of the Oracles of Delphi are known to have survived since classical times, of which over half are said to be historically accurate .

At times when the Pythia was not operating, consultants obtained information from the future in other ways at the site, through the casting of lots, using a simple questioning "yes/no" device, or by seeking counsel from dreams.

It would appear that the supplicant to the oracle would undergo a four stage process, typical of shamanic journeys.

* Step 1: The Journey to Delphi —Supplicants were motivated by some need to undertake the long and sometimes arduous journey to come to Delphi in order to consult the oracle. This journey was motivated by an awareness of the existence of the oracle, the growing motivation on the part of the

individual or group to undertake the journey, and the gathering of information about the oracle as providing answers to important questions.

* Step 2: The Preparation of the Supplicant — Supplicants were interviewed in preparation of their presentation to the Oracle, by the priests in attendance. The genuine cases were sorted and the supplicant had to go through rituals involving the framing of their questions, the presentation of gifts to the Oracle and a procession along the Sacred Way carrying laurel leaves to visit the temple, symbolic of the journey they had made.

* Step 3: The Visit to the Oracle — The supplicant would then be led into the temple to visit the adyton, put his question to the Pythia, receive his answer and depart. The degree of preparation already undergone would mean that the supplicant was already in a highly aroused and meditative state due to cannabis and mushrooms, similar to the shamanic journey elaborated on in the article.

* Step 4: The Return Home —Oracles were meant to give advice to shape future action, that was meant to be implemented by the supplicant, or by those that had sponsored the supplicant to visit the Oracle. The validity of the Oracular utterance was confirmed by the consequences of the application of the oracle to the lives of those people who sought Oracular guidance.

There have been many occasional attempts to find a scientific explanation for the Pythia's inspiration. However, most commonly, these refer to Plutarch's observation that her oracular powers appeared to be linked to cannabis and vapors from the Castalian Spring that surrounded her, together with the observation that sessions of prophecy would either take place in, or be preceded by, a visit to an enclosed chamber at the base of the temple. Plutarch had presided over the Delphic Oracle as a priest at the site for a long period. It has often been suggested that these vapors may have been hallucinogenic gases.

In 2001 evidence of the presence of ethylene, a potential hallucinogen, was found in the temple's local geology and nearby springs by an interdisciplinary team of geologist Jelle Zeiphallus de Boer, archaeologist John R. Hale, forensic chemist Jeffrey P. Chanton, and toxicologist Henry R. Spiller. Ethylene in the highest concentrations was found in the waters of the Kerna spring, immediately above the temple. Although in small quantities, currently the waters of the Kerma spring are diverted from the site for use by the nearby modern town of Delphi. Currently, it is unknown the degree to which ethylene or other gases would be produced at the temple should these waters be allowed to run free, as they did in the ancient world.

It also has been shown recently that the temple of Delphi lies exactly on the intersection of two major fault lines, the north-south, Kerna fault and another east-west Delphic fault paralleling the shore of the Corinthian Gulf, and overlies a local geology of limestone with about 20% of its volume made up of layers of bituminous tars rich in hydrocarbons. The Rift of the Gulf of Corinth is one of the most geologically active sites on Earth. Earth movements there impose immense strains on the earth at accompanying fault lines, heating the rocks and leading to the expulsion of the lighter gasses. It has been disputed as to how the adyton was organized, but it appears clear that this temple was unlike any other in Ancient Greece, in that the supplicant descended a short flight of stairs below the general floor of the temple to enter the Sanctuary of the Oracle. It would appear that a natural cleft or chasm at the intersection of fault lines was enlarged to create the adyton off the centre of the temple, and the flowing waters of the underground springs, would accumulate the gas, concentrating it in the enclosed space. Plutarch reports that the temple was filled with a sweet smell when the deity was present:

"Not often nor regularly, but occasionally and fortuitously, the room in which the seat the god's consulatants is filled with a fragrance and breeze, as if the adyton were sending forth the essences of the sweetest and most expensive perfumes from a spring (Plutarch Moralia 437c). "
Only ethylene of all of the hydrocarbons has such an odor.

Inhalation of ethylene in an enclosed space in which the Pythia was separated from the supplicant by a screen or curtain of some kind, it was argued, exposed the Pythia to sufficiently high concentrations of the narcotic gas to induce a mildly euphoric or trance-like state. Frequent earthquakes, produced by the fact that Greece lies at the intersection of three separate tectonic plates, seem to have been responsible for the observed cracking of the limestone, and the opening up of new channels by which hydrocarbons enter the flowing waters of the Kassotis. This would cause the amounts of ethylene emitted to fluctuate, increasing or decreasing the potency of the drug released, over time. It has been suggested that the decline in the importance of the Oracle after Hadrian was in part due to the fact that there had not been an earthquake in the area for a significant length of time.

In the early twentieth century, an anaesthesiologist named Isabella Herb found that a dose of 20% ethylene gas administered to a subject was a clear threshold. A dosage higher than 20% caused unconsciousness. With less than 20% a trance was induced where the subject could sit up, hear questions and answer them logically, although the tone of their voice might be altered, their speech pattern could be changed, and they may have lost some awareness of their hands and feet, (with some it was possible to have poked a pin or pricked them with a knife and they would not feel it). When patients were removed from the area where the gas accumulated they had no recollection of what had happened, or what they had said. With a dosage of more than 20% the patient lost control over the movement of their limbs and may thrash wildly, groaning in strange voices, losing balance and frequently repeatedly falling. In such cases, studies show that shortly thereafter the person dies. According to Plutarch, who witnessed many prophecies, all of these symptoms match the experience of the Pythia in action.

Plutarch said that the Pythia's life was shortened through the service of Apollo. The sessions were said to be exhausting. At the end of each period the Pythia would be like a runner after a race or a dancer after an ecstatic dance. It clearly had a physical effect on the health of the Pythia.

Tantra and the Mediterranean

The cultural influence of Tantric thought and practice, centered in the Indus River valley and the foothills of the Himalayas, stretched as far west as ancient Greece. Plato's teachings made reference to Tantric beliefs about the clarifying power of moving sexual fluids through secret channels in the body, giving rise to "seminal thoughts" – and also finding concrete representation in the caduceus, the symbol of Western medicine, two serpents entwined around a central shaft. This image is well known in medicine.

Speaking about Tantra in Greece, there had been an age old tradition of a temple priestess helping the spiritual seekers with ceremonial sex. This method of transmitting and transforming sexual energy from one person to the other, was kept hidden from the eyes of common masses for a very long time as, the people would not have been able to perceive any spirituality aspect attached to the process and would have termed it as a basic 'animal instinct' or 'lust'. It has been established and repeatedly affirmed by Yogic teachers and scholars from thousands of years that the 'sexual energy' is a part of our Hydra (Kundalini) energy which in itself is a sum total of etheric or life-force energy. This form of energy, as we know, can be used not only for sexual pleasure and procreation but also for facilitating spiritual growth, by making our Chakra system and higher energies fully functional.

Hecate and Sex

Hecate is the goddess that awakens Hydra and is connected with that dark earth energy we call "Chthonic", a power that our culture fears and misunderstands. It is Hecate's power, a dark sexual underworld, serpentine energy. Sex, death and spirit, the three most powerful forces in our lives, are part of the same tide, and our tragedy lies in forgetting the spirituality in these elevated energies.

As much as Hecate rules over "Chthonic" forces, sex and the power of Hydra, Hydra is a pure positive force that has the potential to awaken. This force should not be misused or great spiritual fall concurs. Once Hydra begins the awakening process, the sexual energy that comes from Hydra is meant to awaken the other Chakras. As well with Cannabis, misuse (addiction) becomes detrimental to the spiritual path. All spiritual unacceptables are meant to be used in moderation.

Spiritual Discipline
(Spiritual disciplines are the essence of Hydra awakening)

The Discipline of Hecate Chthonia

The discipline of Goddess Hecate Chthonia is made during the night. The best place for the disciple is the cemetery, where the disciple should perform worship of this wrathful form of Hecate.

Hecate Chthonia, She is Dark Blue, eyes are fierce, wears dirty clothes, with long white hair. Due to old age she has a bend in her spinal chord. A disciple is to repeat 808 times the Chthonia Hymn (listed under step 8) while meditating on the talisman of Chthonia. This should be done on a new moon in solitude, in the cemetery, desert or in the forest by observing fast and remaining silent the whole day and night. *The Discipline of Chthonia* is used for all round success, protection, psychic opening and spiritual upliftment.

Hecate Chthonia Talisman Guidelines:

A Talisman of Hecate Chthonia is an instrument, or a mystical diagram usually best written on copper. It is a technique or path, considered the simplest way through which one can attain one's desires, and fulfill one's wishes. It is said that 'Hecate Chthonia' reside in the talisman and by performing worship of the talisman, one can appease this form of Hecate, remove the malefic effects, and increase the flow of positive influences. Creating the talisman is easy.

.First bathe and prepare your mind for the practice.

.Find a place on the ground or floor facing <u>west</u>, where you will be undisturbed.

.Light the incense.

.Lay a fresh flower and fresh fruit on the altar.

.Place a small sheet of copper in front of your alter.

.Take rain water and sprinkle the water on the copper for purification.

.Then draw this image on copper with black marker. Also write Hecate Chthonia in Theban above the sigil.

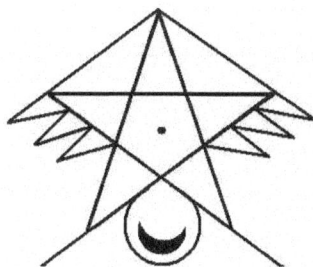

. The Chthonia hymn is to be chanted 17 times after

OH HECATE CHTHONIA, EGO REGINUM TERRIBILEM TRIVIARUM HONORO

Write desire on the back of the sigil.

. Meditate on the image while chanting the invocation (808 times) for full effect as listed on page 160.

Discipline of Hecate Lucifera

The discipline of Goddess Hecate Lucifera is made during the night. The best place for the disciple is a desolate house, abandoned building, or a place where the dead are channeled. This is where the disciple should perform worship of this grave form of Hecate.

Hecate Lucifera, she is grim, eyes are fierce, wears dirty clothes, with black skin. This form of Hecate shifts from maiden to crone. A disciple is to repeat 808 times the Lucifera Hymn (listed under step 8) while meditating on the talisman of Lucifera. This should be done when the moon is in the last 13 degrees of sidereal Scorpio, in an abandoned house, building or at a shine off the road where someone has died in an accident. The worshiper is to refrain from people the whole day and night. *The Discipline of Lucifera* is used for attraction and protection.

Hecate Lucifera Talisman Guidelines:

A Talisman is an instrument, or a mystical diagram usually best written on animal hide. It is a technique or path, considered the simplest way through which one can attain one's desires, and fulfill one's wishes. It is said that 'Hecate Lucifera' reside in the talisman and by performing worship of the talisman, one can appease her, remove the malefic effects of disease, and increase the flow of positive influences.

.First bathe and prepare your mind for the practice.

.Find a place on the ground or floor facing <u>east</u>, where you will be undisturbed.

.Light the incense.

.Lay a fresh flower and fresh fruit on the altar.

.Place a small sheet of animal hide in front of your alter.

.Take rain water and sprinkle the water on the animal hide for purification.

.Then draw this image on the hide with black marker. Also write Hecate Lucifera in Theban above the sigil.

8. The Lucifera hymn is to be chanted 17 times after the image is drawn:

Askei Kataskei eron oreon ior mega samnyer bhaui phobantia semne

Write desire on the back of the sigil.

. Meditate on the image while chanting the invocation (808 times) for full effect.

Discipline of Hecate Luna

The discipline of Goddess Hecate Luna is made during the night. The best place for the disciple is the forest on top of a mountain. This is where the disciple should perform worship of this lunar form of Hecate.

Hecate Luna, she is pleasant, eyes are heavenly, wears white clothes, with midnight blue skin. This form of Hecate is the love of the night. A disciple is to repeat 808 times the Luna Hymn (listed under step 8) while meditating on the talisman of Luna. This should be done under a full moon, in the forest, desert, abandoned house, building or at a shine off the road where someone has died in an accident. Remain silent the whole day and night. *The Discipline of Luna* is used for attraction and psychic abilities.

Hecate Luna Talisman Guidelines:

A Talisman is an instrument, or a mystical diagram usually best written on silver. It is a technique or path, considered the simplest and shortest, through which one can attain one's desires, and fulfill one's wishes. It is said that 'Hecate Luna' reside in the talisman and by performing worship of the talisman, one can appease them, remove the malefic effects of betrayal, and increase the flow of positive influences.

.First bathe and prepare your mind for the practice.

.Find a place on the ground or floor facing north, where you will be undisturbed.

.Light the incense.

.Lay a fresh flower and fresh fruit on the altar.

.Place a small sheet of silver in front of your alter.

.Take rain water and sprinkle the water on the silver for purification.

.Then draw this image on the silver with black marker. Also write Hecate Luna in Theban above the sigil.

.The Luna hymn is to be chanted 17 times after the image is drawn:

Oh Hecate Luna, Ego Reginum Triviarum Honoro
(O Hecate of the Moon, I honor the Queen of the Crossroads)

Write desire on the back of the sigil.

. Meditate on the image while chanting the invocation (808 times) for full effect.

The Discipline of Hecate Triceps

The discipline of Goddess Hecate Triceps is made during the night. The best place for the disciple is the cemetery, where they disciple should perform worship of this wrathful form of Hecate.

Hecate Triceps, she is jet black, triple faced with dog, goat and serpent, eyes are fire, wears black clothes, with long black hair. She is the power of Hydra that resides in the Sex Chakra. A disciple is to repeat 808 times the Triceps Hymn (listed under step 8) while meditating on the talisman of Triceps. This should be done on a new moon in solitude, in the cemetery, desert or in the forest by observing fast and remaining free from people the whole day and night. *The Discipline of Triceps* is used for destroying the "Evil Eye" and for receiving answers in dreams.

Hecate Triceps Talisman Guidelines:

A Talisman is an instrument, or a mystical diagram usually best written on bull or buffalo horn. It is a technique or path, considered the simplest way through which one can attain one's desires, and fulfill one's wishes. It is said that the 'Triceps' resides in the talisman and by performing worship of the talisman, one can appease her, remove the malefic effects of the "Evil Eye", and increase the flow of focused dreaming.

.First bathe and prepare your mind for the practice.

.Find a place on the ground or floor facing <u>south</u>, where you will be undisturbed.

.Light the incense.

.Lay a fresh flower and fresh fruit on the altar.

.Place the horn in front of your alter.

.Take rain water and sprinkle the water on the horn for purification.

.Then draw this image on the horn with black marker. Also write Hecate Triceps in Theban above the sigil, which in this case is the *Wheel of Hecate*.

. The Triceps hymn is to be chanted 17 times after the image is drawn:

OH HECATE TRICEPS, EGO REGINUM TERRIBILEM TRIVIARUM HONORO

Write desire on the back of the sigil.

. Meditate on the image while chanting the invocation (808 times) for full effect.

The Astronomical body of Hecate

(After invoking Hecate, ask her to reside in your body then meditate on your body as hers. This is a common practice in Tantric Buddhist tradition. After years of this meditation, various psychic powers start to develop).

This section deals with the position of the Chakras located in the body of Hecate. The fundamental Chakra is the home of Hecate Brimo, it is of a red color, giving the fruit of all sexuality. Hecate in her serpent form reside's here. The second Chakra is called the Genitalia Chakra, in its center is a vagina, the color is vermilion. In here is the power of creativity, giving the power of all attraction.

Thirdly is the Abdomen Chakra, with five petals, and in its power is of the God Mars. She resembles 10 million Suns, and gives the power of divine sight. The fourth Chakra is the heart-center, with eight petals. Located here is Hecate Lucifera. It is the seat of divine passion, the place where all the senses come to reside.

The fifth is the Collum Chakra, the home of Hecate Trivia, goddess of all mystery. She is the Moon on the right side of her body, and the Sun on the left. In the center is Hydra awakened. One should meditate on the spontaneous sound of the sirens. Above this is the Cerebrum Chakra, it is the Eye of Knowledge. One obtains divine light by meditating here. It is the source of all Light. The sixth Chakra is the home of Hecate Luna, this is the Chakra of Nirvan. It is the color of a column of white smoke. Four inches above this is the Vertex Chakra. Hecate Sol is situated there. If one meditates on this center it gives liberation.

173

Meditating on 16 part of Hecate's body

We will now mention 16 places where the divine meditation of Hecate's body is accomplished. On the tip of the big toe of the right foot one should meditate on a steady light. The second base is situated in the Os Sacrum Chakra, and a flaming fire should be visualized there. Thirdly is the anus, where Hecate's blue fire of Saturn resides. The Fourth is in the sex organ, where the currents of the body are said to come together. Fifth is the tail bone, the tail of Hydra is located here. Sixth is the navel center, in which is the place of divine light, where all sound dissolves. The seventh is the Cor Chakra, where the Mother's breath resides.

The eighth is the throat center. The ninth base is the uvula, at the root of the tongue, whence arises the spiritual bliss. The 10th is behind this, identified with the lower part of the brain. The 11th base is at the tip of the tongue. Meditating here one conquers all disease. The 12th center is the Cerebrum, where one should meditate on the radiance of the moon.

The 13th is the spot at the root of the nose. Meditating here, one becomes concentrated of mind. The 14th base is behind the root of the nose. The 15th is on the forehead, and is the center of light. At the 16th, above the Vertex Chakra, is the Space Chakra, and here reside Hecate Nyx flanked by ghosts and sepernts of fire.

Gods and Goddesses inside the Astronomical Body of Hecate (The Secret Caelums)

Gia is in the genitals. At the base of your genitalia is the Caelum of Saints. These Saints are intoxicated with her bliss. In the heart is a secret chamber called "The Caelum of Typhon." Typhon is one with divine annihilation. The chest region is Lucifera Caelum. The throat region is the Caelum of Minerva. In the center of the throat, in the neck, is the divine mist of intoxication. At the root of the tongue is the Caelum of the river Styx, the river of purifying fire. In the 10th aperture is Bacchus Caelum. Above this 10th aperture is Hydra in her realized form awake in Sol Caelum.

In the forehead is the Heaven without Origin. The Lord Hyperion (Originless One) resides here. At the peak of the head is Soteira Caelum, the residing place of the Queen of "Final" Liberation. In the center of this night is the light of the Absolute. All these forms fall into the body of the "Cosmic Hecate."

The seven underworlds and the heavens all reside in the human body. In the nine apertures are the nine divisions. The seven oceans are identified with the seven main body parts. The spine is **Mount Olympus** and is the aperture at the top of the head. Other mountain ranges exist where there are muscles in the body. The Southern Limestone Alps are on the right ear, and on the left is the Northern Limestone Alps.

The 27 "Palaces" of the Lunar Zodiac dwell in the joints of the hands and fingers along with the smaller mountain ranges. The great rivers are associated with the veins and subtle channels of energy throughout the body. The 12 sidereal constellations light up her hair.

Dwelling in the pores and hairs of the body are the 330 million Angels. Associated with all the Joints of the body and the other places mentioned are the Elements, Ghosts, Daimons and all mystical creatures.

The Sirens, Satyrs, Fairies, serpents of fire and the Ceres also dwell in the body. Her speech is equivalent to the rays of light out spreading in the cosmos. The Parca, and Gorgons dwell in the body as well. Wind is equivalent to breath, and if tears fall it is equivalent to rain.

The lights of consciousness are the Chimera. The Sun and the Moon are the two eyes. The serpent Dracones reside in her legs.

When a person is happy, this is Hecate's happiness. When sad, it is her pain. Free from these distinctions, one is liberated whether asleep or awake. Mother Hecate dwells completely without distinctions in this Cosmos, emanating and shining forth by her own light.

Caelums inside Hecate

Everything exists in Hecate, the seven spheres, earth, sky, planets, the gross plane, the subtle planes and the light reams, the world egg (the primordial mixture of elements), and its elementary envelopes. Hecate's highest influence is the energy of Apollo in Sol Caelum. Although we say the "energy of Apollo" it is Hecate who is the origin of Apollo's energy.

The Cosmic conversation with Hecate

"Oh Hecate, The sphere of the whole earth has been described to me by you, excellent Mother, and I am now desirous to hear an account of the other spheres above the world, the first 4 Caelums and the rest, and the situation and the dimensions of the celestial luminaries. "

"The sphere of the earth, the *Gross Plane*, comprehending its oceans, mountains, and rivers, extends as far as it is illuminated by the rays of the Sun and moon; and to the same extent, both in diameter and circumference, the sphere of the sky the subtle planes spreads above it (as far upwards as to the planetary sphere, or the Mental Planes, *Caelums of light*). The solar orb is situated a hundred thousand miles from the earth; and that of the moon an equal distance from the Sun. At the same interval above the moon occurs the orbit of all the lunar constellations. The planet Mercury is six hundred and fifty two thousand miles above the lunar mansions (Heavenly Palaces). Venus is at the same distance from Mercury. Mars is as far above Venus; and the King of the gods, Jupiter is as far from Mars: whilst Saturn is eight hundred and fifteen thousand miles beyond Jupiter. The sphere of Ursa Major is three hundred and twenty six thousand miles above Saturn; and at a similar height above the pole-star, the pivot or axis of the whole planetary circle.

Above the astral plane, at the distance of two billion miles, lies the sphere of occult masters, or Venus Caelum, the inhabitants of which dwell in it throughout a thousand years which is a day in the high Caelums. At twice that distance is situated Mercury Caelum, where mystics with divine sight reside. At four times the distance, between the two, lies Luna Caelum (the sphere of longing), inhabited by the Arch Angels, who are illumined by fire. At six times the distance is situated Sol Caelum, the sphere of light, the inhabitants of which never again know death !

The region that extends from the earth to the Sun, in which the mystics and other celestial beings move, is the atmospheric sphere, which also I have described. The interval between the Sun and Saturnus Caelum, extending fourteen hundred thousand miles, is called by those who are acquainted with the system of the universe the "heavenly sphere." These three spheres are termed transitory: the three highest, Mercury, Luna and Sol are the places of unlimited bliss. Venus Caelum, is situated between the two. These Caelums, form the extent of the whole universe, I, Hecate have explained to you.

Let me tell you further, the world is encompassed on every side and above and below by the world egg of the original God *Phanes*. Around the outer surface of the shell flows water, for a space equal to ten times the diameter of the world. The waters, again, are encompassed exteriorly by fire; fire by air; and air by Mind; Mind by the origin of the elements and that by Intellect: each of these extends ten times the breadth of that which it encloses; and the last is encircled by the chief Principle, *LIGHT*, which is infinite, and its extent cannot be enumerated: it is therefore called the boundless and illimitable cause of all existing things, Supreme nature, or myself Hecate; the cause of all. Within my life force resides the Soul (Sol), the light of all, diffusive, conscious, and self-radiating, as divine fire. Nature (Gia) and soul (SOL) are both of the character of dependants, and are encompassed by the energy of myself, the great Mother Hecate, which is one with the soul of the cosmos, and which is the cause of the separation of those two (soul and nature) at the period of dissolution; of their aggregation in the continuance of things; and of their combination at the season of creation. In the same manner as the wind ruffles the surface of the water in a hundred bubbles, which of themselves are inert, so the energy of myself Hecate influences the world, consisting of inert nature and soul. Again, as a tree, consisting of root, stem, and branches, springs from a primitive seed, and produces other seeds, whence grow other trees analogous to the first in species, product, and origin, so from the first unexpanded germ (of nature) sprung Intellect and other rudiments of things; from them proceed the grosser elements; and from them men and gods, who are succeeded by sons and the sons of sons. In the growth of a tree from the seed, no detriment occurs to the parent plant, neither is there any waste of beings by the generation of others. In like manner as space and time and the rest are the cause of the tree (through the materiality of the seed), so the divine god Phanes is the cause of all things by successive developments (through the materiality of nature). As all the parts of the future plant, existing in the seed of rice, or the root, the leaf, the stem, the bud, the fruit, the milk, the grain, spontaneously evolve when they are in approximation with the subsidiary means of growth (or earth and water), so gods, men, and other beings, involved in many actions (or necessarily existing in those states which are the consequences of good or evil acts), become manifested only in their full growth, through the influence of the energy of myself.

I, Hecate, am the Supreme spirit, from whence all this world proceeds, who is the world, by whom the world subsists, and in whom it will be resolved. That spirit is the Supreme state of Luna, which is the essence of all that is visible or invisible; with which all that is, is identical; and whence all animate and inanimate existence is derived. I am primary nature: I, in a perceptible form, am the world: and in myself, all finally melts; through me, all things endure. I am the performer of the rites of devotion: I am the rite: I am the fruit which it bestows: I am the implements by which it is performed. There is nothing besides myself, the fully illumined, Mother of all, Hecate."

Light-bearing Hecate (Goddess of Fire)

"Oh Mother Hecate, You have described yourself as the source of all. All elements are within you, but which one holds your power?"

"I am an Underworld Goddess, my connection is fire. Therefore I am called Purphoros (Fire-bearing), Daidoukhos (Torch-bearer), Lucifera (Light-bearer), Puripnon (Fire-breather) and Atra (Black); I am worshiped in caves, deserts, forests and my image is honored with torches.

As a Lunar Goddess I have a complementary relationship to the Sun. At the New Moon, I carry blazing torches and on the new moon, when the Moon is overtaken by the Sun and both rise together, offer my the Amphiphôn (Shining-All-Around), a flat cake with a circle of candles on it. Both Aollo and myself are Gods of the Journey, who illuminate the Way: Apollo by his Sun during the day and my Torch at night. Apollo is also called Hekatos (Distant One), the masculine form of Hekatê (also an epithet of Artemis). Similarly Helios and myself, Mother Hecate, often appear together in magical texts, and we were the only witnesses to the abduction of Persephone. He is the Sun and I am the Moon, the Lamps of Day and Night, the Light Sun and the Dark Sun, Celestial and Chthonic Fire. Ultimately, in the end, all is realized as myself. I create separation and duality so all aspects of myself can be realized by any individual at any moment."

O Lord Helios and Holy Fire, the spear of Hecate Enodia, which She bears frequenting Olympos and dwelling in the Three Ways of the Holy Land. -Homer

In Chaldean Oracles and Neoplatonic philosophers, I am the Womb of Nature, which is fertilized by the lightning and thunderbolts of Father Zeus, and by which I give birth to the physical world. For the lightning bolts correspond to the Platonic Ideas or Forms, which can be embodied only by the mediation of my Womb, the Coils of the Cosmos. These are the thoughts of Typhon, after which is My enwrapping Fire. This Fire, which envelops the world, was called the Membrane (Hymên), and, according to the Oracles, Her Membrane separates the First Fire of the Celestial Father from the Second Fire, which is the Demiurge (Craftsman), Hephaistos. Both are intellectual Fires, one celestial, the other chthonic and proceeding from the first. I nurture the Ideas so that the Demiurge may use them to organize the Elements into our world.

HECATE AND TYPHON

(There are many Hecate truths, Hecate/Typhon is one of them.)

"It is not merely caprice that Skylla's mother is called variously Hecate, Lamia and Echidna in the tradition. All were names of one monstrous being, mother and wife of the giant, dragon-monster whom we know best at Typhon." PYTHON: A study of Delphic Myth and it's origins- Joseph Fontenrose

"Lamia in myth is Scylla's mother, also another name for Hecate or Echidna, meaning viper, seen in her snake form" (Alban 95). "This frightful woman [Hecate ie. Echinda] was spectre, ogress, vampire, snake, sea monster, several kinds of beast and various mixtures of them" (Kabitoglou 311).

Homer and Hesiod called Lamia; Hecate or Echidna. Hecate and Echidna are equated. She was a goddess and frightful one at that. She traveled the world, but "the commonest legend of Lamia places her in Libya." "In Libya there once lived a beautiful queen. Since Zeus loved her and made her his mistress, she aroused Hera's jealousy and hatred. In consequence Hera destroyed every child that was born to Lamia, until from great grief she turned ugly in body and soul." In other words, her despair transformed her into a monstrous creature with evil and vile intentions. "Because she envied other women their children, she went about seizing infants and killing them. Some say that she tore them to pieces or ate them. Finally she became literally a beast and went to live in a cave. Hera sent insomnia upon her too, but Zeus in pity granted her the power to remove her eyes, which she placed in a basket when she wanted to sleep" (Fontenrose 100).

In all of Ancient Rome, Egypt and Greece, Typhon was identified and equated with the Egyptian God of the Underworld, Set. In India, scholars equate Shiva with Typhon. Some attempt to equate Shiva with Bacchus but due to the image of Shiva being greatly whitewashed over the last 100 years this equation

184

falls short. Shiva, originally a funeral god, a destroyer who was described as a withered black man in the cemetery or smashan, became a muscular red headed Mystic of the forest. Shiva's oldest name is Rudra "The Storm God", known as the god of hunting who sat in the lower worlds of Narak (Tartarus). Rudra means "The Howler" and was worshiped by oddiya's (dark magicians). Here is the first known equation of Rudra and Typhon:

Siva, Shiva (Sanskrit) The third god of the Hindu Trimurti (trinity): Brahma the evolver; Vishnu the preserver; and Siva the regenerator or destroyer.

Siva is one of the three loftiest divinities of our solar system, and in his character of destroyer stands *higher than Vishnu for he is "the destroying deity, evolution and PROGRESS personified, who is the regenerator at the same time; who destroys things under one form but to recall them to life under another more perfect type" (SD 2:182). As the destroyer of outward forms he is called Vamadeva. Endowed with so many powers and attributes, Siva possesses a great number of names, and is represented under a corresponding variety of forms. He corresponds to the Palestinian Ba`al or Moloch, the Phoenician, the Egyptian Seth, the Biblical Chiun of Amos, and Greek Typhon.* Shiva: Spiritual - Theosophy Dictionary on, Shiva (SD 2:182)

Typhon's wife, Echidna:

In the most ancient layers of Greek mythology, Echidna (Greek: meaning "she viper") was called the "Mother of All Monsters." Echidna was described by Hesiod as a female monster spawned in a cave, who mothered with her mate Typhoeus (or Typhon) every major horrible monster in the Greek myths, the goddess fierce Echidna who is half a nymph with glancing eyes and fair cheeks, and half again a huge snake, great and awful, with speckled skin, eating raw flesh beneath the secret parts of the holy earth. And there she has a cave deep down under a hollow rock far from the deathless gods and mortal men. There, then, did the gods appoint her a glorious house to dwell in: and she keeps guard in Arima beneath the earth, grim Echidna, a nymph who dies not nor grows

186

old all her days. *(Theogony, 295-305)*

Usually considered an offspring of Tartarus and Gaia, or of Ceto and Phorcys (according to Hesiod) or of Chrysaor and the naiad Callirhoe, or Peiras and Styx (according to Pausanias, who did not know who Peiras was aside from her father), her face and torso of a beautiful woman was depicted as winged in archaic vase-paintings, but always with the body of a serpent. She is also sometimes described as having two serpent's tails. Karl Kerenyi noted an archaic vase-painting with a pair of echidnas performing sacred rites in a vineyard, while on the opposite side of the vessel, goats were attacking the vines: thus chthonic Echidnae are presented as protectors of the vineyard.

The site of her cave, Arima, Homer calls "the couch of Typhoeus" (Iliad, II.783). When she and her mate attacked the Olympians, Zeus beat them back and punished Typhon by sealing him under Mount Etna. However, Zeus allowed Echidna and her children to live as a challenge to future heroes. She was an immortal and ageless nymph to Hesiod (Theogony above), but was killed where she slept by Argus Panoptes, the hundred-eyed giant. Early scholars including Homer equate Echidna was Hecate.

In mystical cosmology, the whole universe is perceived as being created, penetrated and sustained by two fundamental forces, which are permanently in a perfect, indestructible union. These forces or universal aspects are called counterparts.

Tradition has associated to these principles a form, respectively that of a masculine deity and that of a feminine one. Accordingly, Typhon (Rudra in India) represents the constitutive elements of the universe, while Hecate (Kali in India) is the active potency, which makes these elements come to life and act.

From a metaphysical point of view, the divine couple Typhon-Hecate corresponds to two essential aspects of the One: the masculine principle, which represents the abiding aspect of God, and the feminine principle, which represents it's energy, the force which acts in the manifested world, life itself considered at a cosmic level.

Hecate represents the immanent aspect of the Divine, that is the act of active participation in the act of creation. Maybe exactly this mystical view of the Feminine in creation contributed to the orientation of the human being towards the active principles of the universe, rather than towards those of pure transcendence.

Therefore, Typhon defines the traits specific to pure transcendence and is normally associated, from this point of view, to a manifestation of Hecate who is somewhat terrible, a personification of her own untamed and limitless manifestation.

In a way, Hecate is more accessible to human understanding. This may be because she works with aspects of life that are closely related to the human condition inside creation. Hence, the cult of the Goddess has spread more forcibly.

This philosophy promulgates a primordial astronomical duality. From the mystic's perspective, this "scheme" of creation is transformed, in the sense that the two astronomical principles are considered united, not separated. This is the fundamental difference introduced by ancient philosophy, based on a conception that favors the unity between the two principles, opposed in appearance, but indissoluble united in each act of creation.

Nevertheless, mysticism confers to Typhon and Hecate the qualities of the feminine and masculine principles.

The Ecstasy of Hecate and Typhon

Hecate substantiates Typhon's bliss, mysticism's principal objective; hence, mystics resorts to Typhon for his procreative desire for Hecate which is the source of his joy, but to Hecate for all other potentials. The mystic perceives her as multi-aspected, representing, besides female energy, abundance, multiplicity and power to create and destroy. Except in Buddhist tradition, in almost all schools of goddess mysticism, Hecate has a superior status. As Hecate manifests in the 'Wheel of Hecate', the worship of 'Hecate's wheel' is foremost to the mystic. It represents every stage and personality of Hecate. Hence the "Wheel of Hecate" is "Hecate as GODHEAD."

In sexual mysticism (tantra in India) the 'worshiper' attempts to attain the same state of bliss and joy as the unity of Typhon and Hecate. He begins by copulating as his first step. He is the cosmic male, his female counterpart, the cosmic female (or vise versa), and in their ultimate magnification, they are Typhon and Hecate; and, thus, their act of copulation represents the divine union of Typhon and Hecate on a human level. He takes 'cunnus'(vagina) as the manifest form of Hecate, and 'phallus' (penis), as Typhon's, and discovers in the union of the two his means of attaining the ultimate bliss.

Hydra, the daughter of Hecate (Echidna) and Typhon

Hydra, the tool of kindling inherent energies in the Typhon-Hecate myth, is the essence of all spiritual systems. Hydra is the daughter of Typhon and Hecate (Echidna) and the awakening of Hydra manifests through their union. Hydra has been contemplated as dormant energy lying serpent-like coiled in the body. It is a million times more potent than body's known energies, something like the assertion of modern sciences that talk of activating vast dormant areas of the brain which would release incalculable neurological capacities of man. Hence, once Hydra is fully awakened the mystic's consciousness and

Astronomical Consciousness become one. Awakening of Hydra is in the form of its ascent from the 'Root' to the 'Vertex Chakra'.

The body is perceived as comprising six 'Chakras', the active elemental centers, namely, 'Root', 'Sex', 'Navel', 'Heart', 'Throat', and 'Cerebrum'. Over all them is situated the 'Vertex Chakra'–the thousand-petaled lotus. In the 'Os Sacrum Chakra', is an inverted triangular space situated in the midmost portion of the body, it is like a women's vagina in shape. In the center of the lotus is the 'Self manifested-Phallus'. At the base of the 'Phallus' is the divine door, where the Hydra lies asleep. Here itself is the seat of creative desire which, when awakened, pricks Hydra to awake. Thus, the mystic can use intercourse for the awakening of Hydra.

Just above the 'Os Sacrum Chakra' and below the navel is situated the 'Genitalia Chakra', a six-petaled lotus. They represent six qualities or states of being, namely, credulity, suspicion, disdain, delusion or disinclination, false knowledge, and pitilessness. Around the navel is situated 'Abdomen Chakra', a ten-petaled lotus representing ten virtues, namely, shame, fickleness, jealousy, desire, laziness, sadness, dullness, ignorance, aversion, and fear. During 'invocation'or otherwise, the human mind generally inclines to stay in these three 'Chakras'. In true sense it is when the mind enters the 'Cor Chakra' that the journey towards 'Sol Caelum, the Vertex Chakra' begins. The `Cor Chakra', a lotus with twelve petals representing hope, concern, endeavor, sense of arrogance, languor, conceit, discrimination, covetousness, duplicity, indecision, and regret, is situated in the region of heart. Its element is air and here the "self", appears like the flame of a lamp. The Collum Chakra and Cerebrum are situated at throat level and in between the eye-brows respectively in the subtle body. In the Collum Chakra the mystic is in direct touch and contact of godly glory. The 'self'sheds its colors and transcending beyond the material existence dissolves in Sol Caelum. Here and in 'The Cerebrum'it reaches the state of 'Supreme Bliss', a state of complete transcendence.

Hymn to Hecate-Typhon

I offer obeisance to Typhon and Hecate,
The limitless primal parents of the mystic.

They are not entirely the same,
Nor are they not the same.
They are one through their union.

How sweet is their union!
The whole world is too small to contain them,
Yet they live in union in the smallest particle.

These two are the only ones
Who dwell in this home called the universe.

The whole universe is manifested through them,
Everything comes from their union.

When He awakes, the whole house disappears,
And nothing at all is left. Typhon
as Lord resides in Sol Caelum.

Two lutes: one note.
Two flowers: one fragrance.
Two lamps: one light.

Two lips: one word.
Two eyes: one sight.
Hecate/Typhon: one universe.

In unity there is little to behold;
So She, the mother of abundance,
Brought forth the world as play.

He takes the role of witness
Out of love of watching Her.
But when Her appearance is withdrawn,
The role of Witness is abandoned as well.

Through Her,
He assumes the form of the universe;
Without Her,
He is left naked.

If night and day were to approach the Sun,
Both would disappear.

In the same way, their duality would vanish

In fact, the duality of Typhon and Hecate
Cannot exist in that primal state
From which the sound of the sirens emanates.

They are like a stream of knowledge
From which a knower cannot drink
Unless he gives up himself.

So long as unity is undisturbed,
And a graceful pleasure is thereby derived,
Why should not the water find delight
In the floral fragrance of its own rippled surface?

It is in this manner I bow
To the inseparable Hecate and Typhon.

A man returns to himself
When he awakens from sleep;
Likewise, I have perceived Typhon and Hecate
By waking from my ego.

When salt dissolves,
It becomes one with the ocean;
When my ego dissolved, I merge into them.

Hymn to Hecate

Maiden of the Moon Hecate
You are the maiden that
tames all phantoms.

The spirits of the night await
your arrival and dogs
howl in your presence.

You with the black hue
keep all life in balance.

You, Hecate create life
by thought and destroy
it in a single glance.

Tricipitis, Trivia, Inferna,
Vidua, Enodia

Your black mist pours through
the night and the stars bow
at your form.

Hecate, maiden of Lunacy,
maiden of all creatures,
bless me to know your mysteries.
I invoke you as: Oh Hecate Chthonia,
Ego Virginum Cupitatatis honoro

The three deities of Hydra awakening

"Nothing in the spiritual world can be accomplished without Hydra's assistance. The trinity of Hecate, Typhon and Hydra is a mysterious force."

Hecate

Oh Hecate Triceps, Ego Reginum Terribilim Triviarum Honoro

O Hecate of three heads, I honor the terrible Queen of the crossroads

(To be chanted 300 times at the crossroads)

Typhon

Oh Typhoeus, Ego Rexum Terribilim Tempestum Honoro

O Typhon, I honor the terrible King of the storms

(To be chanted 300 times at the on top a mountain)

Hydra

Oh Hydra, Ego Reginum Serpentum Os Sacrum Honoro

O Hydra, I honor the terrible snake Queen of the root Chakra

(To be chanted 300 times while meditating on the root Chakra)

The Goal of the Mystic

The divine mystic is on the path of experiencing God in totality. "The whole universe becomes the body of the Truth-realized Mystic. Others who do not know his real seat or functioning may falsely identify him with his physical body, which they see in front of them with physical eyes. This physical body is only one among the innumerable bodies in which he knows himself as dwelling. His link with this particular body is in no way greater than with other existent bodies in the universe. The Perfect Mystic lives in all and feel equally for all. They can therefore co-ordinate all Divine Work of the Spiritual Hierarchy with wisdom and justice.

It is important to understand how the Universal Body of the Mystic of Sol Caelums stands in relation to other bodies. The gross body is a sort of reflection of the subtle body. It is the exact counterpart of the subtle body. Or we might say that the subtle is a sort of gaseous impression of the gross. Such impression is in a very fine form in the mental body or the mind. The mental body is like a brilliant spark. When the souls, who have attained the supramental Truth, come back, they assume the Universal Mind, which becomes the medium of Hecate's work. It includes and embraces all the existing bodies and pervades the Universe.

The Universal Body of the Mystic of Sol Caelum actually includes, in fact, all worlds and the whole creation. They are all in him. They are all within each soul; but each soul is not conscious of this because of ignorance. It is difficult to believe that huge mountains and forests and towns and even earths and worlds are within, but it is exactly so. The physical eye, which sees all these huge things, is small, yet, it sees them. It does not require huge eyes to see a huge mountain. The reason is that though the eye is small the soul that sees is greater and vaster than all the things which it sees. In fact, it is so great that it includes them all in itself. This does not become clear until the inner mental eye, which really sees through the physical eyes, is inverted.

It is not the physical eye that really sees. It is the mental eye which sees through the physical eye. It is not the physical ear which hears. It is the mind which hears through the ears. This mind, which is most aptly linked to the eye, is ordinarily extrospective, looking outwards and getting bound up with the things that it sees. But when this mental eye is inverted, the universe disappears; and the mind itself becomes the Truth. If the Truth-Mind is again turned towards the universe, it knows itself as permeating and including within its universal body the whole universe.

Through the Universal Body, the Truth-realized Mystic actually finds himself in the minds and the bodies of everyone. It is no difficult task to raise the greatest of sinners to the level of the greatest of saints. The person who plays with the kite and makes it fly freely in the skies, has in his hands the controlling end of the string. He can bring the kite down or allow it to soar as high as he pleases. Likewise, the Perfect Mystic of Sol Caelum is in possession of all the controls of the spiritual evolution of everyone. He has a responsibility to illumine all seven Chakras in others. (3) personal reference

drawing by Maria Magdalene

Removing the Veil of Hecate

Hecate has been generally regarded as the goddess of witchcraft and magic, a crone, Queen of the Underworld or the dark side of the moon. She has been viewed as a women's deity and has been shunned from the patriarchal society. She is considered as Mother of Ghosts, who roams around the graveyard; a merciless killer, who collects poison and embodies death; Bitch or She-Wolf, who howls at night and is followed by barking dogs; and Giver of Vision, who is responsible for insanity (Gimbutas, Living Goddesses 155; Old Europe 198; Kerenyi 36).

There are many other negative, frightening images of Hecate, but such impressions of the goddess can be limiting and misunderstanding of her actual, diverse functions in the ancient world. It is evident that, in many aspects, she signifies "the other side" - the dark, mysterious and fearsome concept, which is referred to as chthonic. Hecate is famously known as a terrifying part of the primordial "Great Goddess", who survives in a form of Hecate-Artemis in Greece. However, it is important to note that she has a dual nature, a quality that is shared by many other Greek and Roman deities. In "Hymn to Hecate" of Theogony (411-52), Hesiod reveals the goddess's positive, powerful and beneficial side. In Chaldean Oracles, Hecate plays a role separate from the ancient feminine principle, being a mediator between theoi and humans. She is also related to and connected with numerous other gods and goddesses, and, through these associations, one can perhaps discern and determine the possible characteristics of Hecate, which may have been forgotten or overlooked. Although many researchers believe that Hecate originates from Caria, southwestern Turkey, it is still a mystery where the goddess exactly comes from. Walter Burkert mentions some researchers' doubts about Hecate's Carian origin, since Lagina, where the main worship for the goddess took place, was all Hellenistic (416). Yves Bonnefoy indicates the possibility of Hecate originating in Egypt, noting that Hecate in male form, which is identified with Apollo, is "the first modern representation of Horus"(262). In the contrary, Robert E. Bell claims that she is from Thrace (219). In Greece, Hecate was often called Enodia, who, in turn, was a goddess of witchcraft and cannabis in Thessaly (Johnston 24). Yet scholars argue that Enodia, who is also called goddess of pathways or she of the roads, has existed independently and separately from Hecate (Burkert 171; Nilsson 91). Despite the controversy, Hecate's origin in Caria seems to be the most solid argument. Burkert points out that the goddess's theophoric name, Hekatomnos, does not fit the Greek language, but it is rather Asiatic, specifically Carian (171). Martin P. Nilsson agrees with Burkert by stating that Hecate's Carian origin has been proven, since researchers have found numerous occasions in Caria, of which the goddess's name appears combined with proper names, while such incidences are quite rare in any other place (90).

In Caria, Hecate was worshiped as one of the most important deities. The most significant temple of Hecate was built in Lagina around 100BCE (Ferguson 160). There, the frieze depicted the stories of Zeus and Hecate side by side, and the goddess was worshiped by sacred eunuchs (Burkert 171; Ferguson 160). In front of the sanctuary, orgiastic dances and games were performed as well as sacrifices of dogs in honor of Hecate (Gimbutas, Living Goddesses 155; Old Europe 197). Hecate Zerynthia was named after Zerynthos, a place that lies west of Lagina (Gimbutas, Old Europe 197). Pausanias also adds, "I know of no other Greeks who believe in sacrificing puppies except at Kolophon, where they sacrifice a black bitch to Hecate" (Guide Vol.2 50). Hecate in Caria might have been closely associated to Cybele, Great Mother of Asia Minor, and her name might have been a name of a daughter of Cybele (Von Rudloff 6). Certainly, Hecate was worshiped outside of Caria as well. The sacrifices of dogs, mysteries and ecstatic dances were also carried out for Hecate in Samothrace, where there was a cave called Zerynthos (Gimbutas, Old Europe 197). Pausanias talks about Hecate in Aegina, where she was honored most of all the gods in a yearly mystery, which was established by Orpheus the Thracian (Mythology 373). Interestingly, in Aegina, Hecate's image, created by Myron, had only one body and a single head (Pausanias, Mythology

374). In contrast, Athenians called the goddess, Hecate Epipyrgidia (Hecate on the Tower), and built the threefold figure of the goddess near the temple of wingless Nike (Pausanias, Mythology 373-74). Hesiod's Theogony is believed to be the first to introduce Hecate in Greek literature. According to Hesiod, Hecate is a Titan daughter of Asteria and Perses, an only child between the star goddess and the son of Eurybia who "shines among all for his intelligence" (375-77, 409-11). One of Hecate's most popular titles, phosphoros, means "the light-bringer" as well as the Greek name for the morning star, implying the goddess's parental heritage (Von Rudloff 4). Phoibe is her grandmother, who, with Koios, has given births to two goddesses, Leto and Asteria; thus Leto's children, Apollo and Artemis are both cousins of Hecate, and they are also called Hekatos and Hecate accordingly (Hesiod 404-9, 918-19; Kerenyi 35-6). Hecate is said to be a reappearance of Phoibe, a great Titan goddess, who is often associated with the moon; and in this relation, Karl Kerenyi finds the poet's attempt to differentiate Hecate the Moon Goddess from Artemis (36). As Kerenyi further investigates, it is true that Hesiod mentions repeatedly about Hecate being the only child or "monogenes", and this notion may indicate the possible resemblance between the conditions and the upbringings of Persephone and Hecate (36). In Theogony, Hecate is "honored above all others" (412) by Zeus. She is given the power over the earth, the sea, and the heaven, "thus exalted exceedingly even among immortals" (Hesiod 415). The famous threefold nature of the goddess might have also been introduced through Theogony in the aspect of Hecate being honored with the three domains of the world (Kerenyi 36).

Except for the subtle and indirect association with the goddess of Hades, Persephone, as being a single offspring, there is no absolute indication of Hecate being unwelcome in male dominant society or feared as a witch by the people of Hesiod's time. Instead of the fierce and baleful image of her, through "Hymn to Hecate", the reader receives an impression of the goddess being equally powerful and celebrated as Zeus. It is possible that she may even be superior to the almighty Zeus, since he cannot forcibly take away her special privileges she has been enjoying among the older generation of gods, the Titans (Hesiod 423-24). It may be that, by Zeus readdressing to Hecate the powers that she has already possessed from the beginning, he is trying to claim the superior authority. Theogony also provides some clues on how the people of the Archaic Greece have perceived the power of Hecate. Hesiod writes that if a man invokes Hecate and sacrifices for her accordingly, he should receive a gift of success (416-20). Hecate is accounted for her authority to grant victory and glory in the battlefield as well as to bring the coveted prize to athletes (Hesiod 430-38). She not only is revered as a fertility goddess for farming products but also contains the power to assist in fishing and horse riding (Hesiod 439-44). Note that "Hymn to Hecate" depicts the goddess as being influential and involved in many productive activities of human life, which are commonly carried out by males. This rather favorable notion of the goddess, Hecate, is sometimes considered as a personal viewpoint of Hesiod and his family. Burkert mentions that Hesiod's family, which originated from Aeolian Cumae, was particularly devoted to Hecate (171). Nilsson says of "Hymn to Hecate", Hesiod's attempt to promote Hecate and establish her as a great goddess, which has ended unsuccessfully (90). Harris and Platzner imply male chauvinism as the main reason for the failure of the propaganda, that the patriarchal society is not capable of accepting a female deity, who is so powerful in many dimensions of human life, except to strip away the positive connotations of the goddess and make her a terrifying witch (101). The only negative quality that is mentioned about Hecate in Theogony is her moodiness or unaccountability. She would supply fishermen with a great amount of fish, but she would also take it away if she wants to do so (Hesiod 442-43). She would side with either side in a war as she wishes, and she can affect the number of livestock animals to reduce or reproduce depending on how she feels (Hesiod 432-33, 445-47). Hesiod emphasizes the goddess's ever-changing mind in his frequent use of phrases such as "at her own pleasure" (446) and "as she pleases" (429). Bell states that Hecate's varying temper may have generated in worshippers' minds a fear; and furthermore this fear has turned into the motivation for the people to revere her (219). Yet this inconsistency in divine character is not only attributed to Hecate but also shared among many ancient deities, and one cannot simply single out Hecate for having the unfavorable trait. It may be possible, provided that Harris and Platzner's assumption is accepted, that this temperament of Hecate, combined with her might, has become the obnoxious, troublesome, dark witch quality that has been rejected by patriarchy. But neither is there adequate evidence nor is it convincing enough to consider this hypothesis as a reasonable contributing factor, which is responsible for creating the negative image of Hecate.

In Homeric Hymn to Demeter, Hecate appears only briefly but plays an important role in Demeter's search for her beloved daughter. She is one of the only two beings in the heaven or on the earth that heard the cry of Persephone besides Helios (Homeric 22-26). Later, Hecate, bringing her torch, comes to see grieving Demeter and tells her what she has heard (Homeric 51-59). She then guides Demeter to Helios, "watcher of gods and men" (Homeric 60-63). When Demeter finally reunites with her daughter, Hecate is also present and, from then on, becomes Persephone's attendant and follower (Homeric 438-40). In the hymn, Hecate is described as "the gentle-tempered daughter of Persaios" (Homeric 24). The gentleness does not fit the popular notion of the goddess being malicious and dreaded, though she residing in a cave indicates chthonicity. Becoming a constant attendant of Persephone in Homeric Hymn to Demeter seems to be the first direct literal connection of Hecate to the Underworld. Sarah Isles Johnston views the goddess's role in the hymn as an intermediary between the upper world and Hades as she accompanies Persephone's annual journey (23). Johnston also points out the association between Helios and Hecate for being the only two immortals, who have noticed the abduction of Persephone (22). Throughout the ancient times, Helios and Hecate had a strong connection when dealing with magic (Johnston 22). It is also true that Helios's companion, Perse or Perseis, the shining Moon, was another name for Hecate, attaching the Underworldly concept to the wife of the Sun (Kerenyi 192).

In addition, the name, Persephone, is a longer, more formal form of such names as Perse, Perseis, Perses, Perseus and Persaios, which are names of Hecate and her relatives (Kerenyi 193, 232). These names have been used from pre-Greek times as a name of the queen of the netherworld (Kerenyi 232). This notion makes more elusive Hecate's original role as well as Hesiod's favorable account of the goddess. Curiously, Von Rudloff suggests that the relationship between Hecate, Persephone and Demeter as the earliest and an indigenous manifestation of Hecate in the triple form (4). He explains the three goddesses as the maiden (Hecate), the bride (Persephone), and the mother (Demeter), who signify the three typical sequential steps of a woman's life in the ancient

Greece (4). This perspective conflicts with that of Harris and Platzner, who place Hecate as the old woman or the crone and Persephone as the virgin (105). This writer found it difficult to define by just reading Homeric Hymn to Demeter whether Hecate was the maiden or the crone; the poet did not indicate anywhere in the hymn which status the goddess represented. Yet in another translation of the hymn, Hecate is depicted as "the childish daughter of Perses" (Rice and Stambaugh 172).

Even though this translation insinuates Hecate being young and chaste, it is a question of how the ancients interpreted the goddess. It seems as though that, from a Hesiodic point of view, Hecate can be seen as a benevolent maiden, while, on the other hand, post-Hesiodic tendency is to assume the goddess to be in the same category as the Gorgons, the Furies and the like. In the discussion of Hecate being the maiden or the old woman, the goddess's connection with Iphigenia gives another clue. In some myths, Agamemnon's virgin daughter, Iphigenia, does not get sacrificed; instead, Artemis spears her life by turning her into a deer, then later into Hecate (Von Rudloff 4). This relationship of Hecate and Iphigenia reinforces the idea of Hecate being the virgin. Hecate had an epithet Baubo in the ancient time (Gimbutas, Language 256). In the Orphic version of the Demeter myth, Baubo and her husband, Dysaules, received Demeter in Eleusis during the goddess's search for her daughter (Bell 93-94; Guthrie 135). The sons of

Baubo and Dysaules, Triptolemos and Eubuleas, witnessed the rape of Persephone and informed Demeter about it (Guthrie 135). Although Baubo served Demeter a drink, the mother of Persephone was in such a grief that she did not accept it (Bell 94; Guthrie 135). Baubo, in her attempt to amuse the sorrowful goddess, lifted her skirt and exposed her rear end (Bell 94). This obscene gesture made Demeter smile, and the goddess finally drank the kykeon (Guthrie 135). This version of Demeter myth offers another different perspective on Hecate. Being linked to Baubo, Hecate manifests a cheerful, friendly and humorous side of her personality. The tie between Hecate and Baubo separates the goddess from the concept of being the maiden; but at the same time, it is highly unlikely that Baubo signifies the older woman.

The name, Baubo, meant "that which she showed to Demeter", the female equivalent of a phallus (Guthrie 135). Hecate as Baubo thus further became an associate of Hermes, whose ithyphallic figures stood in front of gates and doorways (Harris and Platzner 135). Importantly, Hecate's statues and altars were also set up at the entranceways of major shrines, the doorways of houses and crossroads (Burkert 171; Gimbutas, Language 208). Hecate Propylaia meant "the one before the gate" (Von Rudloff 3). During the classical period of Greece, Hecate's name was discussed in various Greek dramas, and through these plays, one could examine how she was regarded by the people of Classical Greece. Aeschylus refers to Hecate in The Suppliant Maidens as Hecate-Artemis, who protect women in their childbirth (676-77). Hecate as a protector of childbirth is also expressed in one of her titles, Kourotrophos. According to Von Rudloff, this title means "child's nurse" and implies not only the governing of the childbirth but also maternal care for all infants (5). Marija Gimbutas further explores Hecate's function in child labor, stating that she, as the Goddess of Death, was believed to devour newborns (Language 219). This rather disturbing act was a symbolic act, which did not connote cannibalism (Gimbutas, Language 219).

Relations in the Greek Pantheon

Hecate is a pre-Olympian chthonic goddess. The Greek sources do not offer a story of her parentage, beyond the Theogony, or of her relations in the Greek pantheon: Sometimes Hecate is a Titaness, daughter of Perses and Asteria, and a mighty helper and protector of mankind. Her continued presence was explained by asserting that, because she was the only Titan that aided Zeus in the battle of gods and Titans, she was not banished into the underworld realms after their defeat by the Olympians. It is also told that she is the daughter of Demeter or Pheraia. Hecate, like Demeter, was a goddess of the earth and fertility. Sometimes she is called a daughter of Zeus.

Like many ancient mother or earth-goddesses she

remains unmarried and has no regular consort. On the other side she is the mother of many monsters, such as Scylla.

Other names and epithets

* Chthonian (Earth/Underworld goddess)
* Crataeis (the Mighty One)
* Enodia (Goddess of the paths)
* Antania (Enemy of mankind)
* Kurotrophos (Nurse of the Children)
* Artemis
* Propylaia (the one before the gate)
* Propolos (the attendant who leads)
* Phosphoros (the light-bringer)
* Soteira ("Saviour")
* Prytania (invincible Queen of the Dead)
* Trivia (latin: Goddess of Three Roads)
* Klêidouchos (Keeper of the Keys)
* Tricephalus or Triceps (The Three-Headed)

Goddess of the crossroads

Hecate had a special role at three-way crossroads, where the Greeks set poles with masks of each of her heads facing different directions. The crossroad aspect of Hecate stems from her original sphere as a goddess of the wilderness and untamed areas. This led to sacrifice in order for safe travel into these areas. This role is similar to lesser Hermes, that is, a god of liminal points or boundaries. Hecate is the Greek version of Trivia "the three ways" in Roman mythology. Eligius in the 7th century CE reminded his recently converted flock in Flanders "No Christian should make or render any devotion to the gods of the trivium, where three roads meet, to the fanes or the rocks, or springs or groves or corners", acts the Druids often did.

Goddess of sorcery

The goddess of sorcery or magic is Hecate's most common modern title. Hecate was the goddess who appeared most often in magical texts such as the Greek Magical Papyri and curse tablets, along with Hermes.

Emblems

Traditionally, Hecate is represented as carrying torches, very often has a knife, and may appear holding a rope, a key, a phial, flowers, or a pomegranate.

The torch is presumably a symbol of the light that illuminates the darkness, as the Greeks secured Hecate in her role as the bringer of wisdom. Her knife represents her role as midwife in cutting the umbilical cord (possibly symbolized by the rope), as well as severing the link between the body and spirit at death. The key is significant to Hecate's role as gatekeeper, being the one who could open the doors to sacred knowledge. The Orphic Hymns list her as the "keybearing Queen of the entire Cosmos." The pomegranate was seen by the Ancient Greeks as the fruit of the underworld, though it was also used as a love-gift between Greek men and women. This may be because a pomegranate was eaten by Persephone, binding her to the underworld and to Hades.

In the "Chaldean Oracles" that were edited in Alexandria, she was also associated with a serpentine maze around a spiral, known as Hecate's wheel (the "Strophalos of Hecate", verse 194 of Isaac Preston Cory's 1836 translation). The symbolism referred to the serpent's power of rebirth, to the labyrinth of knowledge through which Hecate could lead mankind, and to the flame of life itself: "The life-producing bosom of Hecate, that Living Flame which clothes itself in Matter to manifest Existence" (verse 55 of Cory's translation of the Chaldean Oracles).

Animals

The she-dog is the animal most commonly associated with Hecate. She was sometimes called the 'Black she-dog' and black dogs were once sacrificed to her in purification rituals. At Colophon in Thrace, Hecate might be manifest as a dog. The sound of barking dogs was the first sign of her approach in Greek and Roman literature. The frog, significantly a creature that can cross between two elements, is also sacred to Hecate. As a triple goddess, she sometimes appears

217

with three heads-one each of a dog, horse, and bear or of dog, serpent and lion.

During the Medieval period in western Europe, Hecate was reverenced by witches who adopted parts of her mythos as their goddess of sorcery. Because Hecate had already been much maligned by the late Roman period, Christians of the era found it easy to vilify her image. Thus were all her creatures also considered "creatures of darkness"; however, the history of creatures such as ravens, night-owls, snakes, scorpions, asses, bats, horses, bears, and lions as her creatures is not always a dark and frightening one. (Rabinowitz)

Plants and herbs

The yew, cypress, hazel, black poplar, cedar, and willow are all sacred to Hecate. The leaves of the black poplar are dark on one side and light on the other, symbolizing the boundary between the worlds. The yew has long been associated with the Underworld.

The yew has strong associations with death as well as rebirth. A poison prepared from the seeds was used on arrows, and yew wood was commonly used to make bows and dagger hilts. The potion in Hecate's cauldron contains 'slips of yew'. Yew berries carry Hecate's power, and can bring wisdom or death. The seeds are highly poisonous, but the fleshy, coral-colored 'berry' surrounding it is not. If prepared correctly, the berry can cause visual hallucinations (Ratsch).

Many other herbs and plants are associated with Hecate, including garlic, almonds, lavender, thyme, myrrh, mugwort, cardamon, mint, dandelion, hellebore, and lesser celandine. Several poisons and hallucinogens are linked to Hecate, including belladonna, hemlock, cannabis, mandrake, aconite (known as hecateis), and opium poppy. Many of Hecate's plants were those that can be used shamanistically to achieve varyings states of consciousness.

Places

Wild areas, forests, borders, city walls and doorways, crossroads, and graveyards are all associated with Hecate.

Scylla is also the name of a rock on the Italian side of the Strait of Messina, opposite the whirlpool Charybdis. Neither of the names 'Scylla' or 'Charybdis' seem of Indo-European origin. They may be loan words from another culture such as the Minoans or the Phoenicians who were maritime culture.

As Hecate-Artemis, the two goddesses embody the moon cycle as well as the cycle of life - Hecate personifying the end of life, and Artemis representing the youth, purity and the beginning of life (Gimbutas, Language 208). While Artemis is linked with motherhood, Hecate is the Goddess of Darkness; and the act of devouring a child symbolizes that the newborn still belongs to the chthonic darkness even after birth (Gimbutas, Language 219; Old Europe 197). In order for a mother to avoid the Goddess of Death haunting over the life of a newborn, she or the midwife is supposed to destroy all traces of child labor and personally bury in the ground or throw in the ocean the placenta (Gimbutas, Language 219). Gimbutas explains that the placenta is thought to signify the darkness of death; thus discarding the placenta means preventing the child's return to the dark world (Language 219). It is not clear in the short passage of The Suppliant Maidens what Hecate-Artemis in the play is intended to be. Yet Gimbutas's explanation of Hecate-Artemis, especially Hecate as the personification of death and darkness, devouring young children, suggests that the conventional, horrifying portrayal of the goddess has been already established by the Golden Age of Greece. Burkert also notes that Hecate becomes equated with Artemis during the fifth century BCE (171). In the contrary, the resemblance between Hecate and Artemis must have been existed before 700 BCE, since Hesiod tries to separate and distinguish the two goddesses in Theogony, if Kerenyi's account is true on the poet's attempt. As mentioned earlier, Hecate's association with Artemis may be through Iphigenia.

Pausanias, when encountering different stories of Iphigenia in Arkadia, credits Hesiod's poem, Catalogue of Women, as one of the sources that present the story of Iphigenia being turned into Hecate (Guide Vol. 1, 119). One could presume through this information that the link between Artemis, Iphigenia and Hecate was perhaps a Hesiodic understanding of Hecate-Artemis. In Euripides' Helen, Menelaus asks Hecate, the light bearer, to send him better dreams (569). As noted before, Hecate's most common title is phosphoros, the "light-bringer" (Von Rudloff 4). Although many gods and goddesses carried a torch, Hecate was one of the few who had two torches (Von Rudloff 4). She was also considered to be a sender of dreams, especially nightmares. If one has a bad dream and sees a vision of horrifying figures, it is said that he/she is being attacked by Hecate (Nilsson 112). In another play by Euripides, The Medea, Hecate is the personal deity of "the dreaded sorceress" (Burkert 171), as Medea proclaims, "It shall not be - I swear it by her, my mistress, whom most I honor and have chosen as partner, Hecate, who dwells in the recesses of my hearth - that any man shall be glad to have injured me" (395-98).

Von Rudloff believes that Hecate's relationship with Medea, who is often described as a malicious and revengeful foreign witch, has a large impact on creating the goddess's reputation as the instigator of evil, black magic (2). Interestingly, the connection between Hecate and Iphigenia was also related to that of Hecate and Medea, since Iphigenia was called Iphimedeia in the earlier myth of her being saved by Artemis and changed into a deer and then Hecate (Von Rudloff 4). Incidentally, the Black Sea region, where Artemis took Iphigenia for her transformation from a deer to Hecate, was also known to be Medea's homeland (Von Rudloff 4). Also, as Medea says in the quoted passage, Hecate was believed to reside in the extinguished hearth as opposite to Hestia (Roberts 26 Sep.2000). The hearth was probably one time a place for burials, a suitable place to live for the Queen of the Ghosts (Baroja 26). Apollonios Rhodios reemphasizes this bond between Medea and Hecate as well as Hecate's role as the goddess of witchcraft in The Argonautika. She is named Brimo, roarer and rearer, who roams around at night to rule the dead as a chthonian queen (Apollonios Rhodios 3. 861-63). The more detailed illustration of the goddess's figure is given in the story: [Hecate's] whole person was entwined with terrible serpents and oak-leaf saplings; countless torches dazzled and flared, while all around her a pack of clamorous hellhounds bayed shrilly. All the meadows shook at her footfall, and awestruck wailing arose from the nymphs of marshland and river, all those that hold their dances along the meadows of Amaranitian Phasis. (Apollonios Rhodios 3. 1214-20) This is the actual appearance of Brimo whom Jason encounters after his invocation. Hecate's Medusa-like appearance is identified with Gorgon, who also governs the cycle of life and death and represents the Furies side of Artemis, the dangerous woman (Gimbutas, Language 208). In fact, Gorgo is another name for Hecate (Baroja 30). The face of the moon seen by some ancients as the head of Gorgon is undeniably tied to the lunar aspect of Hecate-Artemis (Gimbutas, Language 208).

Medea instructs Jason to invoke the divinity just past midnight by making an offering of the blood of black ewe and honey in honor of the goddess (Apollonios Rhodios 3. 1029, 3. 1031-36; Bell 219). She also advises him to wear a black cloak and never to turn back after the rite, even if he is impelled by howling dogs; otherwise he will not be able to return to his men safely (Apollonios Rhodios 3. 1031, 3. 1038-41). Hecate is being invoked by Jason, for he needs her aid in applying to his skin a magical drug, "the Promethean charm", which Medea has prepared for him (Apollonios Rhodios 3. 843-45, 3. 1211). If smeared on the body, the potion allows the wearer to stay unharmed by spears, be protected from fire, and surpass all others in strength for one day (Apollonios Rhodios 3. 847-50). In The Argonautika, Hecate inevitably appears to be the repulsive old hag rather than the innocent maiden. In this myth, she is also a mother of Scylla by Phorcys (Apollonios Rhodios 4. 828-29). The Argonautika by Apollonios Rhodios assures that, by early Hellenistic era, Hecate has definitely been developed into the deadly, nocturnal divinity, who deals with magic and sorcery. Before investigating more on the aspect of Hecate as the patroness of magic, the word and the concept of magic must be defined in order to comprehend the meaning, in terms of how the ancients understood it. The term, magic or mageia, was originally designated to religious ceremonies, rites and sacrifices that belonged to the Persian culture (Luck 100). These "barbarian" rituals were so different from the Greek traditions that they might have appeared to the Greeks as "magic" (Luck 98, 100). The Persian magoi were priests, who led perhaps the survival of an old worship of the Great Mother (Luck 105). Overall, the term mageia became to be used to refer to the religions of foreign origins; the professional individuals who performed special rites and supplied drugs; or the religious practices that were generally disapproved (Luck 103). Nilsson assumes that the Greeks needed deities, who were closer to them than the Olympian gods, and Hecate was one of the first divinities to be brought from outside of Greece to fulfill the gap between the sky gods and mortals (90, 111). It seems true that magic has enabled the ancient people to be more connected to the external forces and to communicate with the celestial powers more actively, directly and assertively, while formal religious rituals, organized by the state or the community, have only allowed a humble, passive submission of the participants to the higher beings (Luck 96).

Plato, talking about daemons, places magic and communication with the "spirits" as intermediaries between gods and humans; "Through their care goes the whole science of divination, the arts of the priests and of all those concerned with sacrifices in initiations and spells and all divining and witchcraft. God has no intercourse with men: It is through this race that all intercourse happens between gods and men" (qtd. in Luck 103). Magic in Graeco-Roman world can be divided into two categories, namely White and Black Magic (Baroja 23). White Magic was the magic exercised to contribute to the society, such as producing rain, diverting storms, increasing fortune and wealth, treating illness and many other beneficial miracles called on under the daylight in the open area (Baroja 18, 23). Black Magic was summoned for more malevolent purposes, such as wishing to harm an enemy, eradicating someone's crops or livestock, embarrassing a person, interfering a rival from achieving success and ultimately bringing death to someone; and this spiteful magic was done at night in secret places (Baroja 18,23). Hecate is commonly associated with Black Magic, wandering over graveyards on moonless nights, covered in a black mantle, taking joy in watching the blood flow (Apollonios Rhodios 3. 863; Gimbutas, Language 208).

In some myths, she is the mother of Circe and Medea, the two major sorceresses in the ancient mythology (Luck 93). The goddess's name was frequently employed in curse tablets and binding spells, which came into use in the early fifth century BCE through

Hellenistic and Imperial periods (Ogden 4). She was invoked to destroy relationships, to damage assets and fame of another person, to bind someone's soul or to kill a victim (Gager 90, 126-27, 161-62, 183). However, there were many other divinities, besides Hecate, whose names were called upon in these tablets, such as Persephone, Hermes, Hades and Demeter. Hecate's name was also used in more neutral spells, for example, to stop a fight between two people (Gager 212). Even though Hecate's gentler side tends to be forgotten even by the ancients, overtaken by the cruel, fierce characteristics, she can be a charitable practitioner of White Magic, much as Hesiod depicts her; for example, Hecate's torches are held over the fields to assure the fertility of grains (Gimbutas, Old Europe 198). Her beneficial magic is utilized for amulets as well as for healing (Ferguson 101; Gager 222). The deity who can release ghosts and evil daemons can also avert them, and Hecataea, small statues of the goddess, are erected for this purpose (Bell 220; Nilsson 80). One epithet addresses an appreciation to the goddess along with Hermes that these deities have helped a man to be loved by many and succeed as a leader of the mysteries (Rice and Stambaugh 242).

Though her appearances may not be too attractive, Hecate in The Argonautika by Apollonios Rhodios serves as a protector; Medea asks the goddess to protect Jason's life (3.467-68). Hecate also aids her in hypnotizing the dragon, which is guarding the Golden

Fleece (Apollonios Rhodios 4. 147-48). Hecate may be the queen of the deceased souls, but she is also responsible for when the spirit enters the body, that is to say, the process of birth (Baroja 26). She shows a generous quality in Wealth, in which the playwright, Aristophanes, tells the reader that the offerings to the goddess, made by the rich, are taken by the poor so that the poor can survive (594-97). The portrayal of the goddess Hecate seems to have evolved along with the evolution of the concept of magic in the Greek society. During the archaic period, magic was an integral part of life, weaved into ordinary day-to-day activities (Ankarloo and Clark xv). It was so attached to everyday life that nobody questioned anything about magic; magic was tied to philosophical, religious, and other aspects of culture (Ankarloo and Clark xv; Luck 96). Notice that, in the Archaic Greece, Hecate is usually not depicted as a loathsome hag but rather as the strong goddess who embodies multiple dimensions of the world. Later, from around sixth century BCE and onwards, as science and philosophy emerged more independently, the Greek society became divided into two groups - intellectual, "enlightened" minority, which consisted of elites who were too wise to be involved in folk religion, and uneducated, "ignorant" majority, which consisted of general population who stuck with traditional rituals (Luck 96). From this point on, Hecate becomes more and more illustrated as the untamed, vicious female force. Theophrastus, in The Character Sketches, mocks "The Superstitious Man" from the standpoint of Aristotelian philosophy (Luck 97; Theophrastus 16).

The superstitious man, constantly worried, keep washing his hands, sprinkling his body with sacred water, chewing laurel leaves and purifying his house all the time to prevent Hecate from haunting it (Theophrastus 16. 2, 7). Theophrastus goes on to describe the man as extreme and ridiculous, but from the point of view of folk religion practitioners, the character's religious and superstitious acts are considered faithful and devotional, and this pious man can resemble a typical man of Classical Greece, even as early as Hesiod (Rice and Stambaugh 158). During the Hellenistic era, witchcraft or goetic magic seems to have grown more rapidly (Gordon 164). The conflicting point of view is that Hecate, who has been depicted as a ferocious witch, is yet worshiped in Hellenistic Lagina as the most honored deity (Gimbutas, Old Europe 197). As mentioned earlier, the temple to the goddess was built in Lagina around 100 BCE (Ferguson 160). In Caria, Hecate's divine authority seemed to have been equated to that of Zeus (Ferguson 160).

This stance is similar to Hesiod's portrayal of Hecate. Pausanias also notes the reverence of Hecate in Aegina (Mythology 374). It is disputable whether Hecate's worshippers have actually imagined her as the ugly and ill-willed crone (Von Rudloff 6). Although the ancient literature often suggests limited aspects of the versatile goddess, it is quite plausible that, in certain areas of the Mediterranean civilization, Hecate has retained her original, productive power to profit the society. Under the early Roman law code, magic, especially the kind that was employed to hurt others, was more restricted (Gordon 253). In the second century BCE, many men and women were executed for practicing malign magic, though by the first century CE, the citizens' strong need for healing and salvation resulted in the widespread and the intensification of magic (Ferguson 157; Gordon 225; Luck 94). Hecate continued to display herself as the benefactor of ominous witchcraft at this time. Ovid's retelling of Greek myths in Metamorphoses preserves Hecate's threatening, wicked nature, when Circe conjures the forces of Hecate to poison men and turn them into beasts (14. 405). Around this time, myths begin to acknowledge Zeus as Hecate's father, making the goddess more subordinate to the ruler of the sky (Johnston 27). Pheraia was said to be her mother, whose name was an epithet of Artemis (Johnston 27). Hecate was also called Pheraia, and she was abandoned on the crossroads and raised by shepherds (Johnston 27). Hecate later mates with Sky and becomes the mother of Janus, the Roman deity of liminal points (Johnston 27). A chthonic deity, Hecate, as being a daughter to the king of the sky gods, marrying to Sky and giving birth to the god of liminal places is suggestive; perhaps it is symbolizing the interrelation of the contrasting concepts, chthonic and ouranic. The Moon in Roman times was considered to be a mediator between the Sky or the Sun and the Earth (Johnston 30). Actually, Roman sources were the first reliable materials to attach Hecate to the Moon, or they were the only documents surviving, which concreted the idea of Hecate as the Moon goddess (Von Rudloff 4).

During this time, Hecate was identified as Selene and Mene, both were the goddesses of the moon (Bell 397). Simultaneously, Selene was attributed with another name, Phoebe, which is also a name of Hecate as well as her grandmother in Hesiod's Theogony (Bell 397). Hecate-Artemis-Selene as the triple goddess figure was probably a product of the Roman myth (Von Rudloff 4). By the 2nd century CE, the intellectual population of the ancient world - priests and philosophers-were already actively participating in a sophisticated, respectable form of magic, theurgy, in order to be purified and achieve salvation as well as to fight the New Faith, Christianity, and keep the old gods of paganism alive (Flint 285; Luck 95, 101). It should not be mistaken theourgia from goeteia, ("witchcraft"); philosophers distinguished their transcendent mysticism from other "lowly" magic (Flint 285; Luck 99, 101). . The main movement of this sort was Chaldean theurgy, in which Hecate was highly involved as soteira, "savior" (Johnston 1; Von Rudloff 6). Through this magical practice, the participants were enabled to communicate with the supernatural beings, including daemons and dead souls. Hecate, before this time, was thought to hold the keys to open the gate of Hades and release the spirits of the deceased (Johnston 41). The original chthonic ideas on Hecate's keys got broadened by philosophers of late antiquity to be understood as the keys to access every part of the universe (Johnston 42). Moreover, for Chaldean theurgists, Hecate the Moon goddess meant not the mediator between the Heaven and the Earth but the intermediary between the intelligible and physical worlds (Johnston 30). In Chaldean Oracles, Hecate is the Platonic Astronomical Soul, that is, the soul of the Cosmos from which every soul emanates (Johnston 13). In this humble endeavor to understand Hecate, one becomes more and more mystified and confused rather than to visualize the goddess clearly. Gimbutas says of Hecate, "the birth giver and motherly protectress, the youthful and strong virgin, as well as the fearsome and dangerous crone" (Living 155), summarizing the contradictory, controversial, manifold nature of the goddess.

Bell also states that Hecate is perhaps the most complex Greek deity (219). It is safe to say that it would be a mistake to solidify Hecate and categorize her under simplified terms. The general consensus of the divinity as a horrid and hideous witch probably have stemmed from a rather one-sided, conveniently stereotyped re-creation of Hecate, the image which are somewhat detached from the actual deity the ancients worshiped. As each city-state, each community, each family and each individual have envisioned the goddess in their own way, it is possible that there are many more faces Hecate possesses that are yet to be unveiled.

Alexander the Great and Hindu Religion

"The merging of Greece and India has been completely ignored. It is quite possible that India as we know it today was greatly influenced by Alexander the Great. My life's work is now dedicated to the merging of the Ancient Mediterranean and India."- Jade Sol Luna

Alexander the Great (356-323 BC) was depicted in Greek coinage as ram-headed, (Arabic: Zul-Qarnain 'Lord of Two Horns') indicating that he was regarded as a living deity while yet a man. Called in Arabic al-Sikandar or Iskandar, in pan-Indian context the Sikandar name and legend are equally associated with Indian wargod Skanda.

The amazing quests of Alexander the Great startled and thrilled the world. East and West vied with each other in paying him divine honors during his life and after his death. Myths and legends woven around him, embroidered with all the glowing colors of imagination spread through the Continents. The lands he conquered and those beyond them told his tales in diverse tongues. Greek and Latin, Syriac and Arabic,[1] Ethiopic, Hebrew, Samaritan, Armenian, Persian, English and French, German and Italian, and even Scandinavian languages of Europe, Asia, and Africa enshrined in prose and verse the immortal romance of the Macedonian Prince. Those were the days when religion held sway over the minds of men. His tolerance of faiths other than his own, his cosmopolitan outlook in matters religious, inspired as it was by a deep vein of mysticism helped him[2] "wherever he went to treat with respect the local religion." His attitude towards the religion of the Persians, his greatest adversaries, the destruction of their sacred books at Persepolis is one of the rare exceptions to the rule of his general tolerance. The Arabs worshipped him as Iskandar[3] Dhu'lquarnein (two horned Alexander) and even Islam[4] adopted Iskandar among her prophets, and carried his forgotten fame back into India. He was the first Aryan monarch to become a God.[5]

When these various nations with whom he came into contact have preserved various accounts of his life and conquests, have elevated him to the position of a

Superman and God, it is strange, if it be a fact, that Ancient Indian Literature alone is oblivious of him. Great scholars and historians have noted this phenomenon of apparent silence.[6] But they are not surprised. Indians are a peculiar race. India ignores and forgets.[7] "It is a conspiracy of silence." "India remained unchanged. The wounds of battle were quickly healed: the ravaged fields smile again.[8] "No Indian author, Hindu, Jain or Buddhist makes even the faintest allusion to Alexander or his deeds," asserted V.A. Smith, and he quotes with approval the lines by Matthew Arnold:

"The East bowed low before the blast,
in patient, deep disdain.
She let the legions thunder past,
And plunged in thought again."

It is a peculiar theory which holds that man in the East is radically different from members of his species in the West. His skin may be dark or brown, but his normal reactions to external stimuli cannot be different from those of his fellow beings elsewhere. The Sun might shine brighter on him and the hues of land and sky might be more beautiful around him; but the fundamentals of human psychology remain true everywhere. And the vaunted greatness of historians and scholars cannot repudiate the patent facts of the character of 'Homo Sapiens'.

If the Indian mind does not materially differ in

235

fundamental facts, the question naturally arises "Are there allusions or references in Indian Literature to the conquest of Alexander, and if so, what?"

In Persian and Arabic and in Eastern languages generally, it is a well-known fact that Alexander is known under the name of Iskandar. And it is natural, if Indian languages have used his name, it might be a variant of its Asiatic form. What form could it normally assume in the ancient Sanskrit language? We are familiar, through Buddhist sources with the Indianization of the name of the Graeco-Bactrian King, Menander.[9] It occurs as Melinda. On the same analogy, Iskander regularly becomes 'Iskanda.' It is next an easy step to treat the initial 'I' as a case of prosthesis[10] as it obtains regularly in Prakrits, and arrive at the Sanskrit form 'Skanda'. But a suspicion might lurk whether it is not a case of philological legerdemain. The name of Skanda is familiar in Sanskrit, in Indian languages and literature in general. But has it anything to do with Alexander the Great? Is it not an isolated case of accidental coincidence? It behoves us to examine it further.

If there are historical facts of the life and deeds of Alexander analogous to those of Skanda as we gather from the Indian literature and if there is corroboration of material details in the lives of [people?], we have to pause before we reject the hypothesis as idle, far-fetched fantasy.

At the outset, it must be borne in mind that many long centuries have sped since the days of Alexander of Macedon. A tangled mass of myths have grown around his name and eclipsed his true history. The folk-lore of centuries embodying the exploits of local heroes lies entwined over the garbled tales of Alexander, often distorting them beyond recognition. The life of Alexander by a Pseudo-Callisthenes gained unmerited currency and the brilliant hues of lurid fiction threw facts into the shade. We have, then, to extricate historical matter from the cobwebs of age-old legends.

Alexander was a prince, and Kumāra, which means a prince in Sanskrit, is a synonym of 'Skanda.' He was a warlord and leader of an army, and Senānī which means the leader of an army is again a name of Skanda. The lance was Alexander's favourite weapon, and the weapon of Greek soldiers in general, and Skanda is called 'Śakti-dhara' (lance bearer). These are resemblances which may gain weight in the light of other evidences.

The fondest hope and proudest ambition of Philip of Macedon, Alexander's father was to lead a Crusade against Persia after achieving a Pan-Hellenic Confederation. The memories of the incursion of the barbarian hordes from Persia who devastated the smiling lands of Greece and subjugated her inhabitants, were still there in the minds of men. But Philip did not live long enough to see the fructification of his hopes. It was left to his son Alexander to fulfil the dreams of his father. The conquest of Persia and the establishment of a World Empire under Hellenic supremacy was his greatest ambition. The defeat of Darius was perhaps the greatest event of his life. And Skanda was born for the slaying of Tāraka, the asura, who menaced the peace of the world. Now Tāraka is but the sanskritization of Darius[11] 'Dāra' of Eastern legends (Dārayavus of the Persian Inscriptions).[12] Darius in Persian means preserver or protector, and Tāraka in Sanskrit also means preserver or protector. There is at once the similitude of sound and sense. Against the advice[13] of Parmenion, Alexander fired Xerxes's palace at Persepolis as a sign to all Asia that Achaemenid rule had ended. And with the death of Darius and the complete conquest of Persia, Ahura Mazda, the God of Persia was naturally dethroned, and there appeared in his stead the new Aryan God from the West, Alexander. The sway of Ahura Mazda waned with the vanquishing of Achaemenid power. Alexander could legitimately be spoken of as having crushed Ahura Mazda, the guardian deity of the King of Persia. Skanda is referred to as *Mahiṣāsuramardana*. Now *Mahiṣāsura* appears to be the natural sanskritized form of Mazda-Ahura. In the oldest portions of the Avesta, this compound word does not occur in the form of Ahura Mazda.[14] It is Mazda Ahura. But the Sanskrit form is a much-disputed point. Various scholars of repute have essayed at length to arrive at the Sanskrit equivalent of Ahura Mazda. That Asura is the Sanskrit equivalent of Ahura is admitted by all. But controversy crops up, when we come to the equivalent of Mazda.

Dr D.B. Spooner connects it with Maya (Zoroastrian period of Indian History, T.R.A.S. 1915, p. 63-89). The regular Indian equivalent according to the Indologist Dr. Thomas and philologists like Dr. Brugmann (T.R.A.S 1915, p. 78) is *'medha'*. On the strength of a passage in the Rig Veda "*Mahas putrāso asurasya vīrāh*" (Rg. 10.10-12), it is pointed out that Mazda corresponds to Mahas – I venture to suggest that the *Mahiṣāsura* of the *Puranas* is but a Sanskrit rendering of the Mazda Ahura of the Persian, *Mahiṣa* being equivalent to Mazda.

But even in the Vedas, the word Mahiṣa is used in the sense of the great or the venerable. The Uṇādi sūtras derive it by affixing *'ṭiṣac'* to *mah*, (avimahyoṣ ṭiṣac – Unl.48). Jnfiānendra Sarasvati explains Mahiṣa as Mahān and quotes *'turīyam dhāma mahiṣo vivakti'* *'uta mātā mahiṣam anvavenat'*[15] in support of his view; and *Maz* is admittedly the Avestic equivalent of Sanskrit *'Mah'*. Compare also the feminine form *Mahiṣī* which means a queen. The word *Asura* which originally possessed a good signification came to acquire a bad import, probably after the rift between the Persians and the Indo-Aryans.

Alexander married the beautiful princess Roxana the

daughter of the King of Bactria; and Skanda is said to have married Senā or Deva Senā, daughter of Mrtyu according to Skanda Purāna[16] and daughter of Prajāpati according to the Mahā Bhārata.[17] Now it is a well-recognised symbol of language that proper names are contracted in actual usage, and the end often chosen to designate the whole. It was an accepted rule in Sanskrit[18], Kātyāyana says[19] *"vināpi pratyayam pūrvottarapadayor lopo vācyah"* and Patanjali adds *"lopah pūrvapadasya ca."* Senā is but the latter part of Roxana ill-disguised in Sanskrit garb. And the form *Devasenā* is but a Sanskrit rendering with a view to preserving its sense, as Roxana is derived from the root *'raz'* to 'shine' just as deva is from *'div'* to 'shine'.[20] Evidently the king of Bactria is denoted by the word *Mṛtyu*.

On his march into India, Alexander crossed the Hindu Kush mountain through the Koashan pass.[21] The Macedonians who served with Alexander called the mountain Kaukasos,[22] perhaps to flatter Alexander attributing to him the highest geographical adventure, the passage of the Caucasus. The name Hindu Kush is but a corrupted form of 'Indicus Caucasus'. *'Grancasus'* which means 'white with snow' is the original Scythic form of the word Caucasus.[23] Skanda is refereed to as *'Kraunfica dāraṇa'*, and Kraunca is admitted on all hands to be the name of a mountain pierced through by Skanda. Kalidasa refers to this mountain pass as a passage through which swans make their seasonal flights.[24] He but echoes the idea of the Mahābhārata which says *'tena hamsāś ca gṛdhras' ca merum gacchanti parvatam.'*[25] Now *Krauncha* is a more proximate variant of the Grancasus than Kush' is of Caucasus. And the identification of the Kraunch pass with the Koashan is natural and legitimate.

We next come to one of the most interesting facts of history. Chandra Gupta Maurya, the first Emperor of India, while yet a boy, had seen Alexander "the invincible splendid man from the West." "Later on when he became a great King, Chandra Gupta worshipped Alexander among his Gods."[26] It appears a curious fact that a Hindu King paid divine honours to a foreign prince whom he had himself beheld. But the whole world had recognised his divinity. Even the democratic cities of Greece deified and adored him. Egyptian priest had acclaimed him as the son of God and God, and set their seal of assent on the flagrant faith in his divinity. Alexander is said to have visited the temple of Ammon Ra in the oasis of Siwa. He advanced into the mysterious inner sanctuary, and the image declared[27] "Come son of my loins, who loves me so that I give thee royalty of Ra, and the royalty of Horus. I give thee the valiance, I give thee to hold all countries and all religions under thy feet, I give thee to strike all the peoples united together with thy arm."

It was not a notion new to Egypt. "Innumerable empires consecrated to the Sun extended around the

Nile. Millions obeyed the will of one. What the ruler dreamed was fashioned by his slaves with their myriad hands. Everything was possible to him. The King was the son of God…All obeyed him as the descendant of the original conqueror. Because that first conqueror named himself King and son of the Gods, all believed him. Here in the East, it is possible to say to human beings, "I am your God," and all believe."[28] That frame of mind is not the sole monopoly of the East. In the West also that has been the case, and is so perhaps still. Heroes princes and prophets have been deified in the East and the West from time immemorial. The pages of history are strewn with the broken images of God Kings of all times and climes. The elevation of a single man to power without adequate checks leads him to the dizzy heights of megalomania: and people under his power bow before him and pay divine homage; and others take up the thread where they leave it. From Neolithic days when the symbolic sacrifice of a god-king was performed for the fertility of the crop,[29] down to modern times the belief in the chosen man has persisted. The Pharaohs of Egypt, the divine monarchs of Peru,[30] Alexander and Caesar are but a few examples. Dr. Rosenburg, chief of the Department for the Ideological Training of the future German Nation is reported to have said "We need a son of God. Today, there stands among us one, who has been especially blessed by the creator. No one has the right to find fault with those of our people who have found their son of God and have thus regained their Eternal Father."[31] No wonder Herr Hitler, the leader of Germany is being deified.

And in the East, the Dalai Lamas of Tibet and the Emperors of Japan, not to speak of a host of other princes and priests, are living examples of accredited divinity.[32]

The tendency to regard a great and strange foreigner as a god is no less marked.[33] 'The Greeks were quite familiar with the idea that a passing stranger might be God. Homer says that the Gods in the likeness of foreigners roam up and down cities.[34] And, Alexander was no ordinary foreigner. He had captivated the imagination of the world. He himself had a vague faith in his divinity. His followers confirmed it. And Chandragupta might have been influenced by the prevalent craze. His matrimonial alliance with Seleucus who succeeded to the throne of Persia might have made it tactically opportune, and politically expedient. For Indian corroboration, we have the much-disputed passage of Patanjali's Mahābhāsya commenting on Pāṇani's Sūtra *"Jīvikārthe cā'paṇye"* (5-3-99) *"śivah Skando viśākha iti...maurair hiraṇyārthibhir arcāh prakalpitāh."* No one questions the fact that the Mauryas had something to do with the images of Skanda. But who were the Mauryas referred to here? And what did they do? Images are made for worship or for sale or are carried from door to door and alms collected by mendicants. And 'Mauryas' referred to

243

here cannot mean a class of mendicants. The passage is *"Mauryair hiranyārthibhih."* The word *'hiranyārthibhih'* is significant. Beggars do not go about asking for gold. It refers to kings. There are more than half a dozen places in the Mahābhāsya where occurs the sentence *'arthinaś ca rājāno hiranyena bhavanti"* [35] where it refers to a fine or punitive tax collected by kings. The passage might naturally refer to a kind of religious tax collected by the Mauryas and probably introduced by them on the model of the practice of Babylonia where the whole land belonged to God.[36] There might have been periodical religious processions carrying the image of God, when collection was made from house to house. It is a custom that obtains in India even at present. Now Mayūra Vāhana is a synonym of Skanda. He is pictured as riding a peacock. That the Mauryas derive their name from the word 'moriya' which meant peacock and that the peacock was the symbol of the Mauryan dynasty are now facts admitted by scholars of note. The Mahāvamśa Tīkā explains thus the origin of the term Mauryan:[37]

"The appellation of Moriyan sovereigns" is derived from the auspicious circumstance under which their capital, which obtained the name of Moriya, was called into existence.

"While Buddha yet lived, driven by the misfortunes produced by the war of (prince) Vidhudhabo, certain members of the Sākya line retreating to Himavanto, discovered a delightful and beautiful location, well watered and situated in the midst of a forest of lofty bo and other trees. Influenced by the desire of settling there, they founded a town at a place where several great roads met, surrounded by durable ramparts, having gates of defence therein, and embellished with delightful edifices and pleasure gardens. Moreover, that (city) having a row of buildings covered with tiles, which were arranged in the pattern of the plumage of a peacock's neck, and as it resounded with the notes of flocks of 'Konohos' and 'Mayūros' (pea-fowls), was so called. From this circumstance these Sākya lords of this town, and their children and descendants were renowned throughout Jambu dipo by the title of 'Moriya'. From this, the dynasty has been called the Moriyan dynasty."

J. Przyluski says[38] "Mayūra once admitted into the religious literature, had evolved like other Indo-Aryan words. The existence of the Prakrit form 'Mora' explains the nature of the Maurya dynasty. This word which the Chinese translators render by "the family of the Peacock" is to be classed with Mātanga amongst the names of tribes and royal clans related to animal or vegetable." Dr. Radhakumad Mookerji remarks[39] "The connection of the Moriyas or Mauryas with the peacock is attested by interesting monumental evidence. One of the pillars of Asoka shows at its foundation the figure of a peacock, while the sculptures on the great Sanchi Stūpa depict the peacock at three places. Both Faucher and Sir John

Marshall agree with Grunwedel that this representation of the peacock was due to the fact that the peacock was the dynastic symbol of the Mauryas."

Weightier evidences cannot be cited to prove that Mayura or the peacock symbolizes the Mauryas. It is needless to say that the usual deviation based on the assumption that Mura was the name of Chandragupta's mother is ill-founded. As the Mauryas were responsible for the introduction of this worship, and as they might have led the processions carrying the image, Skanda must have come to acquire the appellation of Mayūra Vāhana. It tallies with the evidence of the Mahābhāsya and corroborates western evidence of Chandragupta's Alexander-worship. The identity of the real animal which conveyed Alexander is still preserved in the ritual processions of the image of Skanda mounted on a prancing charger sculptured with realism. The practice obtains generally on occasion of religious processions and particularly when the ritual of a mimic fight between Skanda and the Asura is staged. The Mahabharata corroborates the evidence of the ritual. "Lohitāśvo mahābāhur hiranyakavacah prabhuh." [40] In Margelan of Ferghana, *his red silken banner* is shown even at present.[41] The Mahabharata states, 'Patākā kārttikeyasya Viśākhasya ca lohitā'.[42]

It is an undisputed fact that Alexander was regarded

as the son of God. Even before the oracle of Ammon Ra proclaimed his divine parentage, there were circumstances which tended towards a growing credence in the divinity of his origin. Wheeler remarks[43] "the confidence in an ultimately divine origin was an essential part of every family tree among the noble families of the older Greece. All the great heroes were the sons of Gods. If Minos was the son of Zeus, Theseus must needs, as Bacchylides's paean, XVII shows it, prove himself Poseidon's son." Alexander's mother Olympias who was steeped in the religious mysteries of a semi-Greek land, in the dark cults and orgiastic practices, spells and incantations of primitive religion, made no secret of her conviction that he was the son of god. Even Philip suspected his legitimacy, and the tale went around that the arch-sorcerer Nectanebo, the last Egyptian Pharaoh had visited Olympias in the guise of the ram-headed Ammon and that he was Alexander's real father. Olympias was elated when reports reached her of the oracular confirmation of her conviction. The miraculous success of his military expeditions augmented further the growing belief; and Skanda is referred to as Iśasūnn, the son of God.

Zeus Ammon is often portrayed with the horned head of a ram. And Alexander, the son of Ammon, came to acquire the image of his father with horns springing up from his head. The coinage of Lysimachushas preserved for us the profile of the two-horned god, the Dhulqarnein of the Arabs and their Koran. Chāga

mukha or Chāga vaktra, which means ram-faced, is again one of the synonyms of Skanda.[44]
The Pancatantra (I-45) asks,

"Visnuh sūkararūpena mrgarūpo mahān rsih Sanmukhah chāgarūpena pūjyate kim na sādhubhih"

Alexander was seen in India as an incarnation of Skanda

"Visnu in the form of a boar, the great seer in the form of a deer and Sanmukha in the form of a ram – are these not worshipped by pious men?" It was evidently a popularly known fact expressed by the author of the Panca Tantra fables that Skanda was worshipped in the form of a ram. It might have been so during his days. But who in India knows now of such a worship as that? Who would not be surprised by the epithet chāga-mukha applied to Skanda as we find in the Mahabharata? These are facts that could not be ignored. These are strange corroborations that stare us in the face.

We pass on from the historical facts of his life to the domain of Mythology and Romance to which his name was transported on the wide-spread wings of popular fancy.

"Around him the whole dream-world of the East took shape and substance; of him every old story of a divine world conqueror was told afresh." [45] More than eighty versions of the Alexander-romance, in twenty-four languages have been collected, some of them the wildest of fairy tales; they range from Britain to Malaya; no other story in the world has spread like his. Long before Islam, the Byzantines knew that he had traversed the Silk Route and founded Chubhan, the great Han capital of Sianfu; while the Graeco-Egyptian Romance made him subdue both Rome and Carthage, and compensated him for his failure to reach the eastern Ocean by taking him through the gold and silver pillars of his ancestor Heracles to sail the western. In Jewish lore he becomes master of the Throne of Solomon and the High Priest announces him as ruler of the fourth World-Kingdom of Daniel's Prophecy; he shuts up Gog and Magog behind the Iron Gate of Derbend, and bears on his shoulders the hopes of the whole earth; one thing alone is forbidden to him, to enter the cloud-girdled earthly paradise. The national legend of Iran, in which the man who in fact brought the first knowledge of the Avesta to Europe persecutes the fire-worshippers and burns the sacred book, withers away before the romance of the world-ruler; in Persian story he conquers India, crosses Thibet, and subdues the Faghfur of China with all his dependencies; then he turns and goes northwards across Russia till he comes to the Land of Darkness. But Babylon, as was fitting, took him farthest: for the Babylon-inspired section of the Romance knows that he passed beyond the Darkness and reached the Well of Life at the world's end on the shores of the furthest ocean of them all.

In the hill-state called Nysa, overshadowed by the triple-peaked Mount Meros, probably the modern Koh-I-Mor,[46] Alexander came into contact with the tradition that the Greek god Dionysus was the founder of the city and was the first to conquer India. Arrian tells us that "he heard that the Arabs venerated only two gods, Uranus and Dionysus; the former because he is visible and contains in himself the heavenly luminaries, especially the Sun, from which emanates the greatest and most evident benefit to all things human; and the latter on account of the fame he acquired by his expedition into India. Therefore he thought himself quite worthy to be considered by the Arabs as a third god, since he had performed deeds by no means inferior to those of Dionysus." [47] Was he not himself the accredited son of Zeus? Arrian refers to a current story of Alexander reeling through Carmania at the head of a drunken rout, dressed as Dionysus.[48] Dionysus too is a ram-headed god, the first to conquer India. And the identification is slowly effected. But Mr W.W. Tarn[49] is inclined to suspect the truth of this identification. He says "Thereon, Alexander was deified at Athens, though the story that he became a particular god Dionysus, seems unfounded." He concedes the existence of the story. Only he suspects its authenticity.

The truth of the story of this identification is borne out by the Indian account of Skanda. Most of the ideas current in Greek mythology concerning Dionysus are available in the Indian version. What are the salient features of the conception of Dionysus?

The origins of the cult of Dionysus can be traced to prehistoric times. Dionysus was originally a nature god of fruitfulness and reproduction of all trees and vegetation. Thus in Indian tradition, Skanda is equated with 'Viśākha' or 'Bhadraśākha' (the God of the auspicious or Golden Bough) evidently referring to the deity of vegetal reproduction. These words are remnants reminiscent of the ancient cult of tree-worship, suggestive of Dionysus, Dendrites. Vidyaranya, the philosopher saint speaks of the prevalence of tree-worship which persists even to the present day, in India.

> "Antaryāminam ārabhya sthāvarānteśavādinah
> santy aśvatthā'rka vamśādau
> kuladaivatadarśinah"
> Pancadasi VI, 121

In Europe and Asia, where trees and creepers were worshipped during spring and harvest festivals from the earliest times, a ritual, a symbolic wedding of the tree with some creeper was often celebrated.[50] And poetic imagination everywhere pictured trees and creepers in intimate sexual relation.

> "Paryāpta puspa stabaka stanābhyah
> Spurat pravalostha manoharābhyah
> Latāvadhūbhyas tarvo'pyavāpur
> Vinamra śākhā bhuja bandhanāni"
>   Kumārasambhava

And in South Indian tradition, Skanda, equated with Bhadraśākha (He of the Golden Bough) is represented as marrying Valli, the creeper. The real origin character of this God and his spouse is preserved in tradition as well as in places worship, particularly in Ceylon, where adjoining the temple of Skanda there is a close preserve of cornfield.

Herodotus[51] speaks of Dionysus as a late addition to the Hellenic gods. "Whence the gods severally sprang, whether or no they had existed from all eternity, what forms they bore – these are questions of which the Greeks knew nothing until the other day, so to speak. For Homer and Hesiod were the first to compose theogonies and give the gods their epithets, to allot them their several offices and occupations, and describe their forms."

The worship of Dionysus is said to be of Thracian origin. But the fundamental conceptions underlying the rites and ceremonies of Dionysiac worship are the common heritage of various nations. Yet there is no reason to doubt the veracity of Herodotus's statement that the worship was new to Greece. New forms of ritual and new ideas might naturally have been grafted on to the old existent ones. And that is always the case with religion even when the new one appears to radically differ from the old. The residuum of old faiths remains and through a gradual process of osmosis, diffuses into the new.

The cardinal notions of the cult of Dionysus are evident from The Bacchae of Euripides (Prof. Gilbert Murray's translation),

> "Achelous' roaming daughter,
> Holy Dirce, virgin water,
> Bathed he not of old in thee
> The Babe of God, the Mystery?
> When from out the fire immortal
> To himself his God did take him,
> To his own flesh and bespake him."

In The Bacchae, Dionysus is fire-born and attended by the light of torches. He is Dithyrambos the twice-born: born from fire and again from water. The water-rite or baptism is an ancient ritual. The baptism of fire and the baptism of water are meant for the magical acquisition of strength for the child. And it has survived in Christian ritual to the present day in one form or another.

"In fire is a great strength, and the child must be put in contact with this strength to catch its contagion and grow strong. The water-rite, baptism, has the same intent. Water too is full of sanctity, of force, of 'mana'; through water comes the birth into a new life."

Now we could trace this Bacchic idea in unaltered form even in the Upanisads. The Katha Upanisad says,

"Ya imam madhvadam veda
Ātmānam Jīvam antikāt
Iśānam bhūtabhavyasya
Na tato vijugupsate – etad vai tat
Yah pūrvam tapaso jātam
Adbhyah pūrvam ajāyata
Guhām praviśya tisthantam
Yo bhūtebhir vyapaśysta – etad vai tat."

Katha IV, 5 and 6
"He knows this mead-eater
as the living soul at hand,
Lord of what has been and what is to be,
He shrinks not from him. This verily is that.
He who first from the fire was born
From waters, of old, was born

Who in mystery entered stands,
Who was seen by creatures."

Whatever be the metaphysical interpretation given, the fact remains that there is unmistakable parallelism between these passages from the Bacchae and the Katha Upanisad. The fire-born, water-born mead-eater who stands in mystery cannot escape our notice.

Later Sanskrit literature, particularly classical Sanskrit dramas, abound in descriptions of Vasantotsava or Madanotsava. The Vasantotsava was a regular Bacchanalian festival conforming in all essential details to the authentic western type. Compare the description in the Ratnāvali of Srī Harsa.

> "Preksasva tāvad asya madhu matta kāminījana
> Svayamgrāha grhīta srnfigakajala prahāra nrtyan
> nāgara jana janita kautūhalasya samantatah
> śabdāyamāna mardaloddāma carcarī śabda
> mukhara
> rathyā mukha śobhinah prakīrna patavāsa punfija
> pinjarita daśa diśāmukhasya saśrīkatām madana
> Mahotsavasya."
> Ratnavali, Act. 1

Skanda is frequently spoken of as the son of fire (Agnibhū - the son of the Ganges (Gangāsuta) and Mystery (Guha).

Dionysus us also described as the son of Semele, the

Earth Mother. "He is not only son of Semele, of Earth, but son of Semele as Keraunia, Earth the thunder-smitten."It was appropriate in her case as bride of Zeus, the god of thunder. Euripides has rendered the conception into immortal verse in his Hyoppolytus.

"O mouth of Dirce, O god-built wall
That Dirce's well run under;
You know the Cyprian's fleet foot-fall
Ye saw the heavens round her flare
When she lulled to her sleep that Mother fair
Of Twy-bron Bacchus and crowned her there.
The Bride of the bladed thunder:
For her breath is on all that hath life,
And she floats in the air,
Bee-like, death-like, a wonder"

In the prologue of the Bacchae, Dionysus himself is made to say

"Behold god's son is come unto this land.
of Thebes, even I, Dionysus, whom the brand
of heavn's splendour lit to life, when she
Who bore me Cadmus' daughter Semele,
Died here. So, changed in shape from God to man,
I walk again by Dirce's stream, and scan
[text corrupted]

Now the word Keraunia regularly sanskritized

becomes *saravana*. Compare the analogy of Ionia which admittedly becomes *yavana*. Skanda is Śaravanabhava, born of Śaravana. But the usual Sanskrit etymology of Śaravana a "forest of reeds" seems quite natural, when this original signification was lost through the lapse of time. He is also referred to as *Mahīsuta*, the son of the Earth.

According to Greek mythology, Dionysus, the son of Zeus, was nursed by the nymphs of Pluto. They were originally twelve on number and five of them were placed among the stars as Pluto and seven of them under the name of Pleiades, out of gratitude for their services.

And according to the Indian myth, the six stars *Krttikās* or Pleiades were the nurses of Skanda, and thus he acquired the name of *Kārttikeya*. This particular corroboration is worth noting. The myths are identical. The same star groups figure both in the capacity of nursing nymphs. It is an interesting fact. The constellation of the Pleiades looms large in the imagination of all primitive peoples. The coincidence of the rising or the setting of the constellation with the commencement of the rainy season might have made the primitive man associate these stars with agriculture. This belief was current in both hemispheres. The aborigines of Australia, the Indians of Paraguey and Brazil, Peru and Mexico and North America, the Polynesians and Melanesians, the natives of New Guinea, the Indian Archipelago, and of Africa hold this star-group in veneration. Greeks and Romans and ancient Indians had noted the heliacal rising. Naturally enough, stars which were associated with the rains and the fertility of the crops were regarded as the nurses of the god of vegetation and fertility.

"Dionysus is a god of many names; he is Bacchos, Baccheus, Iacchos, Bassareus, Bromios, Euios, Sabzios, Zagreus, Thyoneus, Lenaios, Eleuthereus, and the list by no means exhausts his titles." Many of them are descriptive titles. "Certain names seem to cling to certain places. Sebazios is Thracian and Phryian, Zagreus Cretan, Bromios largely Theban, Iacchos Athenian."

Zagreus or the Cretan Dionysus is the son of the Goddess Mountain Mother. On the clay impression of a signet ring found at the palace of Cnossos, we come across the figure of the Mountain Mother. On the apex of the mountain, there she stands with two fierce mountain-ranging lions on either side, with an extended weapon, "imperious and dominant." Behind her is her shrine with columns, trident-shaped. The triśūla-shape is unmistakable. Now turn to India. Skanda is the son of Pārvatī Umā. I venture to suggest that Pārvatī Umā is an exact rendering of Mountain Mother. Of course, a curious etymology of Umā has been given by the Puranas, which we find is followed by the great poet, Kalidasa.

"Umeti mātrā tapaso nisiddhā
Pascād umākhyām sumukhī jagāma"
   – Kumāra sambhava

"Forbidden by her mother from penance, with the words "U" "MĀ" (O don't) the graceful girl later acquired the name of Umā."

The ingenuity of the etymology is transparent. In fact, the word *Umā* seems to be related to the Semitic word *'Umma'* which means mother; and *Ambā* and *Ambikā* are other names of Pārvatī.

The worship of a Mother Goddess was prevalent throughout Asia. It obtained in Egypt and from there it is said to have passed on to Greece. Herodotus asserts, "The Egyptians, they went on to affirm, first brought into use the names of twelve gods, which the Greeks adopted from them; and erected altars, images and temples to the gods; and also first engraved upon the stone the figures of animals. In most of these cases they proved to me that what they said was true." George Rawlinson remarks "there is also evidence of the Greeks having borrowed much from Egypt in their early Mythology as well as in later times, after their religion had long been formed." In Egypt we find a Goddess "standing on a lion, like 'Mother Earth' who is mentioned by Macrobius (Saturn. I, 26). We find her again in Assyrian monuments. The very name of the Egyptian Mother Goddess is *'Maut'*. The comments of the great scholar G. Rawlinson on this point are again worth quoting. "Besides the evidence of common origin, from the analogies in the Egyptian, Indian, Greek and other systems we perceive that Mythology had advanced to a certain point before the early migration took place from central Asia. And is in after times each introduced local changes, they often borrowed so largely from their neighbours that a strong resemblance was maintained; and hence the religions resembled each other, partly from having a common origin, partly from direct imitation, and partly from adaptation; which continued to a late period." But whether the early migration took place from Central Asia or not is a question beyond the purview of this book.

We have already referred to Dionysos being portrayed as ram-headed and Skanda being Chānga-mukha. It is interesting to note, in this connection, that he is referred to as '*Naigameya*' in the Mahabharata. Would it not be possible that this word has its origin in misreading and mis-spelling the word *Nysian*, Dionysos being taken to mean the Nysian God. Such a suspicion is strengthened by the large variety of forms in which the word Naigameya occurs in various works. It occurs as *Nejamesa* in the Grhya Sūtras of Āśvalāyana and Śānkhāyana, as *Naigamesa* in Suśruta and as *Nemeśa* in the Mathurā Inscription. Professor Pargiter gives various illustrations of flagrant misreadings of names. *Naiśeya* or *Naiśayeya* meaning Nysian would have easily assumed all these various forms.

The Indian legend concerning the origin of Skanda is vague, vacillant and divergent. Different sources give different tales. The Mahabharata has two or three varying versions. The tone of dubious hesitancy is patent. The first version of the story goes that Vasistha and the other Rsis were offering a sacrifice. Agni, being invoked, descended from the Sun, entered into the fire and received the oblations. Issuing forth from the fire, he beheld the lovely spouses of the seven Rsis, bathing pleasantly in their hermitages. They shone like golden altars, pure as the crescent moon, like the flames of fire, and all as wondrous as the stars. The mind of Agni was upset. He became the slave of his passion. Knowing no other means of quenching his lust, he entered into the domestic fire and beheld them and touched them with his flames. Thus he dwelt for long enamoured of these lovely women. But his heart's desire was unfulfilled, and in distress and despair, he decided to abandon his corporeal form and retired into the forest. Now Svāhā, the daughter of Daksa has fallen in love with him. Her amour was unrequited and she now found an opportune moment and a clever ruse. She assumed the form of the wives of the six rsis, one after another, and enjoyed the bliss of union with Agni. But she was not able to impersonate Arundhati, the chaste wife of Vasistha. Thus,

> "six times was the seed of Agni thrown into the reservoir on the first of the lunar fortnight. Discharged there and collected, that seed by its

energy generated a son. That which was discharged (Skanna) being worshipped by the rsis became Skanda."

(Vanaparvan Ch. 227)
"Sātkrtvatas tu niksiptam
Agne retah kurūttama
tasmin kunde pratipadi
Kāminyā svāhyā tadā
tat skannam tejasā tatra
samvrtam janayat sutam
rsibhih pūjitam skannam
Anayat skandatām tatah."
Vanaparvan, Ch. 227 (17-18).

It is evident that Śiva or Rudra does not come in here, nor do the Krttikā stars. In the next stage, Agni is equated with Rudra and the Krttikās are slyly smuggled in.

"Brahmins call Agni Rudra; therefore, he (Skanda) is the son of Rudra. The seed which was discharged by Rudra became the white mountain. And the seed of Agni was placed by the Krttikās on the white mountain. All the devas having seen him honored by Rudra, they call him who is the mysterious one, the best of the virtuous, the son of Rudra. This child was born when Rudra had entered the fire. Skanda, the greatest of the Devas, was born with the energy of Rudra, of Agni, of Svāhā and of the six

262

women. Therefore he became the son of Rudra."

Vanaparvan Ch. 229 (35-38)

"Rudram agnim dvijāh prāhuh
rudrasūnus tatas tu sah
rudrena śukram utsrstam
tat śvetah parvato' bhavat
pāvakasyendriyam śvete
krttikābhih krtam nage
pūjyamānam tu rudrena
drstvā sarve divaukasah
Rudrasūnum tatat prāhur
guham gunavatām varam
Anupraviśya rudrena
Vahnim jāto' hy ayam śiśuh
tatra jātas tatas skando
rudraunus tatō' bhavat
rudrasya vahneh svāhāyāh
Sannām strīnām ca tejasā
jātas skandas suraśrestho
rudrasūnus tato' bhavat."
Vanaparvan Ch. 229 (35-48)

The confusion arising out of the attempt at the fusion of different concepts is hardly disguised. We perceive the very process of fusion, the trembling fingers of the fabulist at work, mixing and mingling divergent legends. Rudra and Agni, Svāhā and Krttikās are all jostling against each other. The introduction of the Krttikās does not appear to serve a purpose here. The acquisition of the six faces through their intrusion is mentioned only later. And there, Śiva has slowly displaced Agni from his original fatherhood. Agni becomes the agonized bearer of Śiva's caustic energy.

"The discharged energy of Śiva fell into Agni. The Lord Agni was not better able to bear all that imperishable stuff. The brilliant bearer of oblations was sinking under it. Being advised by Brahma, he deposited it in the Ganges. The Ganges herself incapable of bearing it threw it ashore on the venerable Himalayan range. There, the son of Agni grew encompassing the worlds. The Krttikās saw that lustrous foetal form in the thicket of Sara reeds, and each one cried out "he is mine." The lord knowing their maternal affection drank the effluent milk of their breast with six mouths."

Śalyaparvan, Ch. 45 (6-12)

"Tejo māheśvaram skannam
Agnau prapatitam purā
tat sarvam bhagavān agnih
nā' śakad dhartum akśayam
tena sīdati tejavi
dīptimān havyavāhanah
na ca'inam dhārayāmāsa
brahmane uktavān prabhuh
sa gangām upasangamya
niyogād brahmanah

264

garbham āhitavān divyam
bhāskararopamatejasam
atha gangā'pi tam garbham
asahantī vidhārane
utsasarji girau ramie
himavaty amarārcite
sa tatra vavrdhe lokān
āvrtya jvalanākāram
dadrśur jvalananākāram
tam garbham atha krttikāh
śarastambe mahātmānam
analātmajam īśvaram
mamā'yam iti tāh sarvāh
putrārthmyo' bhicukruśuh
tāsām viditvā bhāvam tam
mātrnam bhagavān prabhuh
prasnutānām payah sadbhir
vadanair apibat tadā."
      (Salyaparvan, Ch.45 (6-12)

Finally we get a summary of results:

"Some regard him as the son of Brahman,
some as the eternal boy, the eldest born,
some as the son of Śiva, and some as the
son of Agni, of Umā, of Krttikās and of the Ganges."

      Salyaparvan, Ch.45 (98-99).
Kecid enam vyavasyanti
pitāmahasutam prabhum
sanatkumāram sarveśam

265

brahmayonim tam agrajam
kecid maheśvarasutam
Kecit putram vibhāvasoh
Umāyāh krttikānām ca
Ganfigāyāś ca vadanty uta
(Salyaparvan Ch. 45 (98-99)

We are now going to tread on more controversial ground. Dionysus is said to be the son of Zeus and Skanda is the son of Siva. Could it be that the very word Siva itself is an Indianization of Zeus and imported from outside? The word Zeus has a long history behind it. Philologists are agreed that agreed that Zeus is the Greek form of the Sanskrit word *"dyaus"* which means sky, and we have the form *"divas pitr"* corresponding to the western from Zeus-pater or Jupiter. But the word Siva in the sense of a god, we do not come across in the Vedas. We are familiar with Rudra, the Vedic counterpart of the Puranic Siva. We meet Siva in some Upanisads, the chronology of which is questionable. Pānani is familiar with Siva, and Patanjali too. That is to say, earlier than the 4th Century B.C., the usually accepted date of Panini, three is no authentic mention of Siva. It is not proposed here to claim Siva to be a thorough-bred foreigner. The excavations at Mohenja Daro have brought to light a seal (Plate XII of Sir John Marshall's work) representing a prototype of Siva Paśupati, and it reveals the hoary antiquity of such a conception. As so often happens in the history of religion, new names and new notions were overlaid on the old. But a question might naturally arise. If the word Siva has come from Greece, how could Pānini be aware of him in the 4th Century or thereabout? India had come into contact with the western world, long before the conquest of Alexander. From the days of Xerxes who invaded the North-West, India had frequent intercourse with the West. Contingents of Indian troops had served in the armies of Xerxes and Darius in their expeditions against Greece. Trade and commerce might have helped the process of the diffusion of religion and culture. But it is rather a hazardous venture to hang on the frail form of a verbal resemblance in matters like this. But the parallelism does not stop with the word.

Attributes of Siva with which we are familiar in Indian religious literature are discernable in the case of his Greek counter-part Zeus. We note Zeus as Jupiter triophthalmos the triple-eyed god. Siva as triambaka is worshipped throughout India; and triambaka is always explained as three-eyed. We become aware, for once, of the fact, that there is a word *amba* or *ambaka* in Sanskrit which means an eye. It is suspicious.

In Egypt we encounter the Solar god variously called Atin, Atys, or Attin, who was both male and female (Macrobius-Saturn I, 26). We meet the double-sexed god again in Europe. Says Rawlinson,

"Macrobius (Saturn III.7) speaks of a bearded Venus

in Cyprus and She is called by Aristophanes 'Aphroditos', apparently according with the notion of Jupiter being of two sexes, as well as of many characters and with the Egyptian notion of a self-producing and self-engendering deity. This union of the two sexes is also found in Hindoo mythology, and similarly emblematic of the generative of productive principles." Of course, the double-sexed Zeus of Hindu Mythology is Siva, Ardhanārīśvara. It is a striking similarity.

Herodotus speaks of a Jupiter Stratius worshipped by the Carians.

"He was also called Jupiter Labrandeus, either from his temple at Labranda or from the fact that he bore in his right hand a double-headed battle-axe ('Labra' in the Lydian language). Such a representation of Jupiter is sometimes found upon Carian coins. And a similar axe appears frequently as an architectural ornament in the buildings of the country."

Here we are naturally reminded of Siva as Khanda paraśu figuring so frequently in Sanskrit literature.

It is an admitted fact that the word 'Tues' of Tuesday is derived from the name of the old German God Zio, (Zeus) or Tius. The Indian names of the days of the week are exactly corresponding to the western names. These names assuredly, had a common origin. Dion Cassius expressly states that the seven days were first

268

referred to the seven planets by the Egyptians. The 'tues' of Tuesday appears as *Cevva* in Dravidian languages. That is as much as to say that the Dravidian word Cevva corresponds to the western word Zeus. Now in Tamil, the alleged root of the word Cevva may be spelt either way as *'Civ'* or *'Cev'*, and C is pronounced as Ś. If this process of reasoning is sound, it would follow that, while directly through Vedic and Sanskrit, various forms of the word *'dyaus'* became current in India, it reached India again through the Greek form Zeus, after circuitous migrations in diverse lands, passing through diverse tongues. This fact explains the absence of the God Siva in the Vedas, and probably South India hugged to her bosom this new-come god with fervid devotion. Of course, there were gods and goddesses too before the arrival of Siva. But again, they paled into insignificance before the impetuous new-comer. The conception of Siva as astamurti is a bold attempt at an all-embracing symposium of diverse allied cults of the worship of Zeus, as the Sun, the moon, etc. Even the practice of the devotees of Siva daubing themselves with white ashes (*bhasman*) is analogous to the orphic rite of the worshippers of Zeus besmearing their bodies with dust or ashes or gypsum which the ancients called *'titanos'*. Archbishop Eustathius commenting on the word Titan says,

"We apply the word titanos in general to dust, in particular to what is called asbestos, which is the

white fluffy substance in burnt stones."

It is claimed by some that Skanda is purely a South Indian God and there are no Skanda temples in the north. It might be so or not now. But even during the days of Kalidasa, we come across great Skanda Shrines of note in the north. Cf. *'Tatra skandum niyatavasatim'* – Meghadūta. Sānkarācārya invokes him as the God of the Indus region.
Cf. Subrahmanya Bhujanga:

> *iIti vyanfijayan sindhutīre ya āste*
> *tam īde pavitram parāśaktiputram."*
> *"namas sindhave sindhu deśāya tasmai*
> *punas skandamūrte namas te namo' stu."*

Before the introduction of the Skanda or Kārttikeya cult from the north, under the name of Subrahmanya, South India was paying for her divine homage to Muruka, amongst other local primitive deities. Amongst Dravidians it was a very ancient worship. But even here, palpable affinities could be traced to similar religious rites elsewhere. Muruka, like Skanda, is the God of War. He was also the God of Hunting. We are told of a Babylonian and Cushite God of Hunting and of War under a name variously spelt as Murik, Mirukh and Mirikh. Murik is really the original Cushite and it is still applied by the Arabs to the planet Mars which has always represented the God of War: and does even today represent Skanda in India. The word occurs still in this vernacular form in

Ethiopian inscriptions. The worship of the same god with the same functions under the same name by apparently different races is a problem for ethnologists to tackle. But the fact remains. Either the Cushites and Dravidians might both belong to the same race, or one might have adopted the practice from the other. The former is the more probable hypothesis.

Theocrasia, or the fusing of one god with another has played a conspicuous part in the history of religion from prehistoric times. In the oldest Egyptian religion, Horus, the son of God Osiris (Serapis) was regarded as the intercessor with the Father for sinners. H.G. Wells says,

> "Many of the hymns to Horus are singularly like Christian hymns in their spirit and phraseology. That beautiful hymn "Sun of my soul, thou Saviour dear", was once Sung in Egypt to Horus. In this worship of Serapis which spread very widely throughout the civilized world in the third and second centuries B.C., we see the most remarkable anticipations and usages and forms of expression that were destined to dominate the European world throughout the Christian era. The essential idea, the living spirit of Christianity was, as we shall presently show , a new thing in the history of the mind and will of man; but the garments of ritual and symbol and formula that Christianity has worn, and still in

many countries wears to this day, were certainly woven in the cult and temples of Jupiter-Serapis and Isis."

The cult of Skanda was super-imposed on the Muruka cult. But the ancient form of worship persisted. With slight modifications, it exists to the present day.

When Dionysos first came to Greece – from where exactly we do not know whether from Thrace or elsewhere – he came with a vast train of attendants; his revel rout of Satyrs and Centaurs and Maenads. "The Centaurs, it used to be said, are Vedic Gandharvas, cloud-demons. Mythology now-a-days has fallen from the clouds, and with it the Centaurs." Homer alludes to them as *"wild men, mountain haunting."* On the metopes of the Parthenon, they appear as horses with the head and trunk of a man. *"By the middle of the 5th Century B.C., in knightly horse-loving Athens, the horse-form had got the upper hand. In Archaic representations, the reverse is the case. The centaurs are in art what they are in reality, men, with men's legs and feet, but they are shaggy mountain-men with some of the qualities and habits of beasts, so to indicate this in a horse-loving country, they have the hind quarters of a horse tacked on to their human bodies."*
Satyrs were essentially akin to the Centaurs. But when the Centaurs evolved in mythology from wild men to become more and more horse-like, the Satyrs retained their characteristics of wild men with diverse

beastly adjuncts. The Maenads are the women-attendants of Dionysos, his nursing nymphs, in mythology. Maenad means 'mad woman'. In actual ceremonial, they were women worshippers possessed, maddened or inspired by his spirit. They had various titles, *"Maenad, Thyiad, Phoibad, Lyssad",* meaning "Mad one, Rushing one, Inspired one, Raging one." These Satyrs and Centaurs and Maenads correspond to the Sattvas (bhūtas) and Kinnaras and Mātrganas of Indian Mythology. The Bhūtaganas retain, in India too, the same mischievous and frolicsome Puck-like traits of their Greek counter-parts. The Kinnaras appear with palpable corporal inversion. Their trunks are human, but the heads are horse-like, and they are frequently referred to as *aśva mukhas* ('having horse-face'). The Mātrganas figure prominently in the Mahabharata and the Puranas. The women who were seized with divine frenzy when possessed by the God have left traces of their vanishing existence in ancient Tamil poetry, though they have faded out of the social life of modern times in India.

These Maenads or nursing nymphs were represented, as we know, by *"frenzied sanctified women"* who worshipped Dionysus as a baby in his cradle. In this particular form, Dionysus came to be called 'Dionysus Liknites' – *Liknon* meaning a cradle. The Orphic ceremonial of the Liknophoria or the carrying of the Liknon was widely practiced in Greece. Votive offerings of various sorts, originally the first fruits of the earth and often the best of things dear to man were carried in the Liknon to the shrine of Dionysus.

The kāvadi in South India is almost the representation of an Indian cradle, carried topsy-turvy by the devotee on his shoulder with offerings hung from the horizontal pole. The word *kāvadi* means, in Tamil *"a decorated pole of wood with an arch over it carried on shoulders with offerings, mostly for Muruka's temple."* In a vase-painting from a Krater in the Hermitage Museum at St. Petersburg, we get an exact representation of the modern Indian kāvadi – the outline of an arch covered with fillets, curving over the ends of a horizontal pole with foliar decorations, placed under the feet of Dionysus. Dr. J.E. Harrison, the talented of the author Prolegomena' and 'Themis', regards this representation as the Omphalos of Gaia, the earth Goddess, the mother of Dionysus. But, the Earth Goddess does not appear in the picture, and the filleted arch is under Dionysus's feet. Whatever that be, its resemblance to the kāvadi is striking and noteworthy. How was Dionysus worshipped in Ancient Greece? Exact details of mystic rites cannot possibly be had. But we get interesting descriptions.

"His worshippers, women especially, held nightly revels in his honour by torch-light on the mountain tops. Dancing in ecstasy to the sounds of cymbals and drums, they tore in pieces a sacrificial animal, whose blood they drank with wine."

In Athens, the worship of Dionysus was later

reformed by Epimenides and was purged of certain objectionable elements. Dr. J.E. Harrison quotes a dialogue between Pentheus and Dionysus.

> P. How is this worship held, by night or day?
> D. Most oft by night, 'tis a majestic thing
> The darkness.
> Ha! With women worshipping.
> 'Tis craft and rottenness."

Herodotus speaks of the maddening influence of Dionysus. The band of raving revellers seized by the god go dancing in divine frenzy. The scenes were similar in India. The veteran scholar Mr. P.T. Srinivasa Iyengar says,

> *"The god of the hilly region was the Red God (Seyon) also called Murugan, who was the patron of prenuptial love. He was offered by his worshippers balls of rice mixed with the red blood of goats killed in his behalf. He was a hunter and carried the Vel or Spear...This god created a love-frenzy in girls."*

He quotes again from the Pattinapālai, 11. 134-158, and translates:

> "In the market streets there were ceaseless festivals to Murugan, in which women, obsessed by him, danced, and the flute, and the Yāl [lute] were sounded and the drums beaten."

We behold today with our own eyes, around us here, pious devotees of Skanda dancing in ecstasy to the rhythmic beat of resounding drums. We cannot afford to ignore the unchanging persistence of this very ancient cult. Men may come and men may go, but it seems, the cult goes on for ever.

I have attempted to show that the very name Skanda is a foreign importation, that many prominent features of the Skanda cult are immigrants. Different strata of beliefs could be distinguished in the conglomerate mass of myths and legends woven around Skanda. Various races and ages have left the impression of their diverse contributions. Egyptian, Babylonian, Cushite, Dravidian and Greek and Indo-Aryan conceptions of a particular form of divinity have all coalesced into a complex faith. Each has impressed its indelible seal in its present form. Since the advent of Alexander, old faiths took a new turn, assumed a new cloak. That new trend is discernable. I have but advanced here a few evidences which go to prove my contention.

But there could be a serious objection. If the word *Skanda* has been introduced into India after Alexander's conquest, Indian literature before the days of Alexander could not possibly refer to him. Are there not references in the pre-Alexadrine literature of India? There is no mention of Skanda in the Vedas. But it occurs once in the Upanisadic literature. In the Chāndogya Upanisad, a seer of the name Skanda Sanatkumāra is mentioned. It must, first, be noted that it is not a god Skanda yet, that is referred to. Secondly, the chronology of the Upanisads and of Vedic literature in general first stated by the Max Muller and accepted by the majority of the scholars is open to grave doubts. Thirdly, the passage where it occurs has been alleged to be an interpolation by competent authorities.

The problem of Vedic Chronology is one of the most intricate problems of Sanskrit literature. Chronology is, in general, the weak point of the Indian Literary history. Whitney in the introduction to his Sanskrit grammar said *"all dates given in Indian literary history are pins set up to be bowled down again."* Those words ring true even today.

Max Muller started from the few known facts of Indian history – the Invasion of Alexander, and the rise of Buddhism in his chronological theory. His arguments were as follows:

1. Buddhism is nothing but a reaction against Brahminism and it presupposes the existence of the entire Veda Samhitas, Brāhmanas, Āranyakas and Upanisads. Therefore, it must have arisen before 500 B.C.

2. Vedānga and Sūtra literature probably arose simultaneously with the origin and early spread of Buddhism. These works may be placed in the

period from 600 to 200 B.C. But the Sūtra works presuppose the Brāhmanas. For these he set apart 200 years. Thus the Brāhmanas came to be dated from 800-600 B.C.

3. The Brāhmanas in their turn, presuppose the Samhitas. Let 200 years be allotted for the arrangement of the Samhitas. Thus the Samhitas were arranged from 1000-800 B.C.

4. But arrangements could not take place before composition. Another 200 years for composition. This Veda were composed during the period from 1200-1000 B.C.

5. The arguments, indeed, are simple. But from the starting point of the Sūtra period fixed during 600-200 B.C. through the generous and uniform intervals of 200 years, his hypothesis flounders on. And Max Muller himself had no absolute faith in his theory. He says, in his Gifford lectures on Physical Religion, *"Whether the Vedic hymns were composed 1000 or 1500 or 2000 or 3000 years B.C., no power on earth will ever determine."* But those who followed him would not leave his theory forlorn. When he vacillated, his followers took it up in right earnest and said that he could not go back, they would support him. That is in short, the story of Vedic Chronology.

The premise that Buddhism presupposes the entire

Veda from Samhitas to Upanisads can hardly be held. In fact the earliest Upanisads like the Brhadāranyaka and the Chāndogya show, let alone the later ones, traces of Buddhistic influence. Dr R. E. Hume, the learned translator of the thirteen principal Upanisads says:

"Yet, evidence of Buddhistic influence is not wanting in them. In Brhadāranyaka 3-2-13 it is stated that after death the different parts of a person return to the different parts of nature from whence they came, that even his soul (ātman) goes into space and that only his Karma, or effect of work remains over. This is out and out of the Buddhist doctrine. Connections in the point of dialect may also be shown. Sarvāvat is a word which as yet has not been discovered in the whole range of Sanskrit literature, except in Śatapatha Brāhmana and in Northern Buddhist writings. Its Pali equivalent is sabbava. In Brh 4-3-2-6 'r' is changed to 'l', i.e. palyayate from pary-ayate -- a change which is regularly made in the Pali dialect in which the books of Southern Buddhism are written...Somewhat surer evidence, however, is the use of the second person plural ending 'tha' for 'ta'. Muller pointed out in connection with the word acaratha (Mundaka 1-2-1) that this irregularity looks suspiciously Buddhistic. There, however, four other similar instances."

In reference to the Chāndogya Upanisad, Prof. Keith says *"By a division, which seems to have no precedent in Brahmanical texts, and which has certainly no merit, logical or psychological, the individual is divided into five aggregates or groups (khandha), the Sanskrit equivalent of which means 'body' in the phrase Dharma skandha in the Chāndogya Upanisad. "Trayo dharmaskandhāh"* (Chāndogya 2.23).

Beck compares it with the Dīgha Nikāya passage, where the three imperfect conceptions of self as body, as mind and as ideas are referred to.

The Upanisads, it must be noted, mark a break from the tradition of Vedic sacerdotalism. It is not a normal and regular development of the speculation of the Samhitas, what little there is. New thoughts and new theories radically opposed to already existing forms, strike us at every turn. Ritual acts are condemned. Priests are ridiculed. The new and sublime doctrine of the soul and again the doctrine of transmigration appear here, for the first time. The Ksatriya is elevated, often, above the Brahmin. It is a revolt. It is as much a revolt as Buddhism. Buddhism was the expression of the revolt of a master mind against the darker forces of the world, against the inequalities of life, against the thraldom of a rigid social hierarchy, against dirt and sin and slavery. Whenever in the history of human thought, we find an abrupt break, a swift swerve from the regular course of normal evolution, the impact of a master mind will be evident somewhere. That came from the Buddha. But it is possible that the Buddha himself represented the normal reaction of a different race against the incursion of new Aryan tendencies. And Upanisadic literature reflects the tendencies of that new spirit. The hypothesis usually held, that Buddhism presupposes the Upanisads seems ill-founded. The converse might be nearer the truth.

There are scholars like Hopkins and Jackson who place the bulk of the Rg Veda hymns between 800 and 600 B.C. on the evidence of the very close affinity of the contents and language of the Rg Veda and the Avesta.

But, whatever be the chronology of the Upanisads, it is admitted on all hands that the two Upanisads Brhadāranyaka and Chāndogya are of a composite character. Different books have been strung together – ill-strung though – to give us the present versions. And naturally enough, interpolations easily creep in.

If certain notions of the deification of a great foreign prince have been incorporated into legends concerning an Indian God it need not perturb us. The Bhagavad Gītā assures us –

"Ye Yathā mām prapadyante
tāns tathaiva bhajāmy aham"
and Gaudapāda says:

"Yam bhāvam darśayed yasya
tam bhāvam sa tu paśyati
tam cā'vati sa bhūtvā sau
tadgrahah samupaiti tam."
        Kārikā II, 29.

The fountain-head of all religions is the pure and devout heart of man, thrilled by the awe and mystery of the universe. The stream might course through diverse regions, carrying with it the various tributes of minor streams. But it cleanses and refreshes and strengthens all that seek it, and moves onwards to its final goal, the vast and mysterious ocean.

    Bahudhā' pyāgamair bhinnāh
    panthānah siddhihetavah
    tvayy eva nipatanty oghā
    jāhnavīyā ivā ' rnave
        Kālidāsa's Raghuvamśa

The culture and civilization of India have always been assimilative. India, at heart knows no distinction of East and west. Well and truly has the noble Marquess of Zetland said:

"The legacy of India, how rich a heritage, drawing contributions, as it does, from diverse races and from many epochs both preceding and following the great Aryan incursion from the lands lying beyond the snow-capped ranges of Hindu Kush"[52]

SKANDA ŚATKAM

Skandah kumārah senānīh
Śaktibhrd raktaketanah
Aśvārūdhas tārakārir
Mahiśāsuramardanah
Devasenāpatir devah
Kraunficarandhravidāranah
Mayūravarasamsevyah
Sindhu deśa samādrtah
Naigameyaś chāgavaktro
Madhvadi vahninandanah
Apām suto dvijo divyo
Guhah śaravanodbhavah
Mahyā umāyāh pārvatyās
Tanayah krttikāsutah
Vallīvrto bhadraśākho
Bhūtakinnarasevitah
Nānāvāditra kuśalair
Nānā lāsya vilāsibhih
Bhaktamātrganaih sevyo
Murukaś śivanandanah
Ābrahma stamba samvyāpto
Yo brahmanyah sanātanah
Sankalpa kalpavrksāya
Tasmai sarvātmane namah

Sources

1. *Alexander the Great* by Wheeler

2. *Ancient India* by M. Crindle (Calcutta-1936).

3. *Ancient Indian Historical Tradition* by Pargiter.

4. *Arrians Anabasis of Alexander* by E.J. Chinnock.

5. *Bacchae of Euripides* by Prof. Gilbert Murray.

6. Brhadāranyaka Upanisad.

7. *Buddhist Philosophy* by A.B. Keith (Oxford.)

8. *Cambridge Ancient History* Vol. VI.

9. Chāndoyga Upanisad.

10. *Classical Dictionary* by Sir William Smith and G.E. Marindin, New Impression, 1919.

11. *Early History of India* by V.A. Smith, (Oxford, 4th edn.)

12. *The Encyclopaedia of Religion and Ethics*.

13. *The Golden Bough* of Frazer.

14. *Herodotus* (Rawlinson's) (Vol. I-IV).

15. *A History of Ancient Sanskrit Literature* by Max Muller, (Allahabad-1912)

16. *A History of the Ancient World* by Rostovtzeff.

17. *A History of Sumer and Akkas*, by L.W. King.

18. *A History of the Tamils* by P.T.S.

19. *The House of Seleucus* by E.R. Bevan.

20. *India in Greece* by E. Pococke.

21. *India, What it can teach us* by Max Muller.

22. Katha Upanisad

23. Kumārasambhava.

24. *The Legacy of India* (Edited by G.T. Garrat).

25. Mahabharata (Bombay-1908).

26. *Mahābhāsya* of Patanjali.

27. Meghadūta.

28. Milindapanfiha.

29. *Napoleon* by Emil Ludwig.

284

30. *New Light on Ancient Egypt* by G. Maspero.

31. Odyssey.

32. *The Origin and Development of Religion in Vedic Literature* by Dr. P. S. Deshmukh.

33. *The Outline of History* by H. G. Wells – 7th revision 1932.

34. Pancatantra.

35. *Philip and Alexander of Macedon* by Hogarth.

36. *Plutarch's Lives.*

37. *Pre-Aryan and Pre-Dravidian in India* by Dr. P. C. Bagchi.

38. *Proceedings and Transactions of the First Oriental Conference.*

39. *Prolegomena to the Study of Greek Religion* by Dr. J. E. Harrison – 2nd Edition, 1908.

40. Ratnāvali of Sri Harsa.

41. *Religions of India.*

42. *Religion and Philosophy of the Veda* (2 Vols.) by A. B. Keith.

43. Rgveda.

44. Siddhānta Kanmudī(i) with Tattvabodhinī (Bombay, 1908.)

45. *Skanda Purana* (Bombay, 1908)

46. *S. K. Aiyangar Commemoration Volume.*

47. Sophist of Plato.

48. Subrahmanyabhujanga of Sri Sankaracarya

49. Sunday Times (Madras).

50. *Tamil Lexicon* – Madras University.

51. *Themis* by Dr. J. E. Harrison.

52. *The Thirteen Principal Upanisads* (Translated by Dr. R. E. Hume).

Hecate Extras

Hecate Iphimedeia- Under this name she is consort to Neptune.

Styx- Hecate is identified as the Goddess Styx all throughout Hesoids Theogony. Furthering her as the Goddess of the underworld and fire.

Nepthys-to go against popular belief, I do not believe that Hecate comes from the Egyptian goddess Heket, as the Greek meaning of the name Hecate and the Egyptian meaning of Heket are so vastly different. I have always associated Hecate to Nepthys.

Nephthys defined:

*In Egyptian mythology, **Nephthys** is the Greek form of an epithet (correctly spelled **Nebet-het**, and **Nebt-het**, in transliteration from Egyptian hieroglyphs). Nephthys, therefore, is a member of the Great Ennead of Heliopolis, a daughter of Nut and Geb. Nephthys was the divine corresponding "power" (or completion) of her sister, Isis and, in a somewhat lesser fashion, the sister-wife of Set. Nephthys is occasionally regarded as the mother of the funerary-deity Anubis.*

Nephthys apparently was known in a wide spectrum of ancient Egyptian temple theologies and cosmologies as the "Useful Goddess" or the "Excellent Goddess" [1]. In this sense, late ancient Egyptian temple texts prove to be pointedly accurate depictions of a far more nuanced goddess, one who represented divine assistance and protective guardianship on a multitude of levels.

A more certain understanding in regard to this divinity has been hampered necessarily due to the fragmented aspect of ongoing efforts to document and publish specific temple (and other inscriptional) discoveries, excavations, and theologies, along with relatively few concerted attempts to draw various and disparate strands of evidence into some form of cohesive whole. In this regard, the work of E. Hornung [2] has proved to be revelatory, along with the work of several noted scholars (see below, passim).

Perhaps most interestingly for our current consideration, Nephthys was not at all restricted to the purely passive or formless status so often accorded to her by various commentators.

On the contrary, Nephthys quite often is featured as a rather ferocious and dangerous divinity, capable of incinerating the enemies of the <u>Pharaoh</u> with her fiery breath [3]. As the primary "nursing mother" of the incarnate Pharaonic-god, <u>Horus</u>, Nephthys also was considered to be, de facto, the mightiest nurse of the reigning Pharaoh himself [4]. Though many goddesses could arbitrarily assume this role, depending upon the local setting, Nephthys was ostensibly and nationally, irreplaceable in this function. It is important, within this framework, to appreciate the potency of the Osirian Royal-Mortuary-Deity cults (and their primacy) in understanding exactly how the chief Osirian deities exercised enormous influence in widespread, fundamentally crucial temple rituals and practices from <u>Dynasty V</u> and beyond.

Certainly with the coming of the <u>New Kingdom</u> Ramesside Pharaohs, in particular, one witnesses a royal lineage enamored of Mother Nephthys, as is attested in various stelae and a wealth of inscriptions at Karnak and Luxor. Nephthys was a member of that great city's Ennead—just as she was in Heliopolis— and her altars were present in the massive complex [5]. An inherited reverence for protective qualities made Nephthys a goddess of notable flexibility who did not, as is often stated, live constantly in the

288

shadow of her great sister, <u>Isis</u>. Moreover, Nephthys was one of the few national goddesses to serve as <u>tutelary</u> divinity of her own district, or nome, in Ancient Egyptian history. Indeed, Upper Egyptian Nome VII and its city, Hwt-Sekhem, were considered (at least by Greco-Roman times) to be the unique fiefdom of Nephthys [6].

Nephthys is a goddess of undetermined origin, but contrary to many erroneous claims, her ancient Egyptian name did not mean "Lady of the House," as if referring to an ordinary human home. She was not in any way to be identified with some notion of a "housewife," nor as the primary lady who ruled the common domestic household. This is a pervasive and egregious error, oft-repeated, in very many commentaries concerning this deity. Rather, her name means quite specifically, Lady of the [Temple] Enclosure.

This title (which seems to be more of an <u>epithet</u>, rather than a goddess-name) likely indicates the association of Nephthys with one particular temple or some specific aspect of the Egyptian temple that is now partially lost to modern understanding. We do know, from a wealth of sources (cf. P. Wilson, above), that (along with her sister Isis) Nephthys represented the temple <u>pylon</u> or the great <u>flagstaff</u> heralding the Divine Dwelling. Due to her very streamlined role as a protective entity, we may even consider the simplest

289

explanation in which Nephthys truly lives-up to her unique epithet and is to be identified with the fundamentally protective temple enclosure-wall itself. All other efforts to determine the exact origin of this goddess remain speculative. To reiterate, her name seems to be an epithet masking the original, sacred name of this divinity (whatever it was). Sacred names were kept secret. She may well have been artificially created by Heliopolitan theologians to serve as a counterpart or doppelganger of Isis, but the specific nature of her epithet "Mistress of the [Temple] Enclosure" mitigates against this, and the idea remains speculative.

By the time of the <u>Fifth Dynasty</u> <u>Pyramid Texts</u>, Nephthys appears as a goddess of the <u>Heliopolis</u> cosmic family. She is the counterpart, or twin, of Isis and, in more surprisingly cursory fashion, features as an almost nominal companion of the war-like deity, <u>Set</u>. As sister of <u>Isis</u> and especially <u>Osiris</u>, Nephthys is a blatantly protective goddess who symbolized the transitional death experience, just as Isis represented the transitional birth experience. In the funerary role, Nephthys often was depicted as a kite or <u>falcon</u>, or as a woman with falcon wings, usually outstretched as a symbol of her protective proclivities. She was, almost without fail, depicted as crowned by the hieroglyphics signifying her name, which were a combination of signs for the sacred temple enclosure (hwt), along with the sign for neb, or mistress (Lady), atop the enclosure.[7]

In the <u>Pyramid Texts</u> Nephthys is unquestionably a great, ubiquitous, and yet enigmatic presence. Normally she appears in potent congress with her sister, Isis, as a fortifying entity. She is one of the Nine Great Ones of <u>Heliopolis</u>. Nevertheless, she also turns up as the companion of Set in a few key passages. Because Set represented the stark aridity of the desert in ancient Egypt, he was generally viewed as a sterile deity in myth and in temple cult. Therefore, Nephthys was, in most districts, seen as a childless entity as well. Myths that portray Nephthys as the mother of Anubis are either latecomers to the body of ancient Egyptian lore or vague allusions.

Nephthys's early association with the kite or the Egyptian hawk (and its piercing, mournful cries) evidently reminded the ancients of the lamentations usually offered for the dead by wailing women. In this capacity, it is easy to see how Nephthys could be associated with death and putrefaction in the <u>Pyramid Texts</u>.

Even so, in the <u>Pyramid Texts</u>, Nephthys possesses attributes of an ominous nature that make of her personality something occasionally unique, in comparison to Isis. Indeed, the hair of Nephthys is compared, in one curious passage, to the strips of linen that enshroud the deceased Pharaoh's mummy. These "tresses," however, are not considered to be bonds. On the contrary, they appear as life-giving and temporary impediments from which the Pharaoh is encouraged to "break free" and ascend to the afterlife. It is no great leap (in terms of symbolism) to see that the "tresses of Nephthys" here assume a role very much akin to the chrysalis-shell that simultaneously immobilizes and yet protectively transforms the caterpillar before it bursts forth into new life. To be certain, there is absolutely no overt comparison, in the Pyramid Texts, between this function of Nephthys and the chrysalis, but the symbolism is one that may merit further exploration of Nephthys's unique domain, since the aforementioned passage is one of only eight (in the Pyramid Texts) wherein this goddess appears independent of her complementary power, Isis.

Whatever the scenario, Nephthys was clearly viewed (in the above-noted example) as a morbid-but-crucial force of heavenly transition, ie., the Pharaoh becomes strong for his journey to the afterlife by breaking free from Nephthys. The same divine power could be applied later to all of the dead, who were advised to consider Nephthys a necessary companion. According to the Pyramid Texts, Nephthys, along with Isis, was a force before whom demons trembled in fear, and whose magical spells were necessary for navigating the various levels of Duat, as the region of the afterlife was termed.

It should here be noted that Nephthys was not necessarily viewed as the polar opposite of Isis, but rather as a different reflection of the same reality: eternal life in transition. Thus, Nephthys was also seen in the Pyramid Texts as a supportive cosmic *force occupying the night-bark on the journey of <u>Ra</u>, the majestic <u>sun god</u>, particularly when he entered <u>Duat</u> at the transitional time of dusk, or twilight. Isis was Ra's companion at the coming of dawn. The union between the Two Sisters cannot be overemphasized. At the same time, their distinct polarities cannot be dismissed.*

[edit] Nephthys and Set

Though it commonly has been assumed that Nepthys was married to Set, recent Egyptological research has called this into question. Levai notes that while Plutarch's De Iside et Osiride mentions the deity's marriage, there is very little specifically linking Nephthys and Set in the original early Egyption sources. She argues that the later evidence suggests that:

while Nephthys's marriage to Seth was a part of Egyptian mythology, it was not a part of the myth of the murder and resurrection of Osiris. She was not paired with Seth the villain, but with Seth's other aspect, the benevolent figure who was the killer of Apophis. This was the aspect of Seth worshiped in the western oases during the Roman period, where he is depicted with Nephthys as co-ruler. [8]

[edit] The Saving Sister of Osiris

Nephthys - Greco-Roman era painted image on a linen and tempera shroud - c. 300-200 B.C. - Metropolitan Museum of Art

Isis - Greco-Roman era painted image on a linen and tempera shroud - c. 300-200 B.C. - Metropolitan Museum of Art

Nephthys plays an important role in the rudimentary Osirian myth-cycle (as delineated in the Pyramid Texts) and even more so in the temple cults that steadily arose across the length and breadth of ancient Egypt from this particular body of myth.

It is Nephthys who appears as the force of dual completion, assisting Isis in gathering and mourning the dismembered portions of the body of Osiris, after his murder by the envious Set. These acts of "gathering" and "mourning" were not mere pedantic motifs, much in the same way that Osiris's role as a scattered corpse cannot be seen as an entirely passive or meaningless divine emblem. On the contrary, these acts on the part of Nephthys and Isis were inordinately powerful and effectual: the "gathering" and "mourning" were efforts that genuinely altered the chasm between Life and Death—these acts energized and empowered "The God" (Osiris), and hence the complete life-cycle of the Nile, for the preservation of the very balance between Order and Chaos.

Why Nephthys was so firmly entrenched in Osirian loyalties (when she also is clearly associated with Set) is a conundrum. Her original prerogatives may indeed, have been sequestered within the framework of a sort of power-dyad with Isis for the ritual gathering, unification, and magical resurrection of Osiris, but the ancient Egyptian lore masters apparently were not afraid of contrast. Nephthys is the companion of Set, yet she also is the interested, reliable, and devoted "Saving Sister of the God [Osiris]", who completes the resurrectional equation with Isis. (In a most basic fashion, the abundant information regarding the Osirian myth-cycle, whether from the Pyramid Texts, the Metternich Stela, or the musings of Plutarch, and such, should be *considered as pertinent sources for the first three portions of this article).*

Thereafter, Nephthys also serves as the primary nursemaid and watchful guardian of the infant Horus, often in the absence of (or in apposition to) Isis herself. It is no small matter that the above-mentioned sources (including the Pyramid texts) refer to Isis as the "birth-mother" and to Nephthys as the "nursing-mother" of the totemic Pharaonic deity (Horus). Above all else, the magical power of Nephthys was viewed as the necessary fulfillment of the power of Isis, and vice versa. Interestingly, though Nephthys was attested as one of the four "Great Chiefs" ruling in the Osirian cult-center of Busiris, in the Delta (cf. The Book of the Dead, Theban Recension), she appears to have occupied only an honorary position at the holy city of <u>Abydos</u>. No cult is attested for her there, though she certainly figured as a goddess of great importance in the annual rites conducted, wherein two chosen females or priestesses played the roles of Isis and Nephthys and performed the elaborate <u>Lamentations of Isis and Nephthys</u>—an almost liturgical collection of songs that formed a crucial part of a sort of Passion Play in honor of the God. There, at Abydos, Nephthys joined Isis as a mourner in the hallowed cenotaph shrine known as the Osireion (cf.Byron Esely Shafer, Dieter Arnold, Temples in Ancient Egypt, p. 112, 2005). Moreover, these "Festival Songs of Isis and Nephthys" were *ritual elements of many such Osirian rites in major ancient Egyptian cult-centers.*

Without doubt, in fundamental ancient Egyptian myth and temple cult, it is only as a duo that the "Two Sisters" (Isis and Nephthys) are equipped to reunite, reconstitute, and resurrect the body of Osiris. Thereafter, both goddesses (or one in place of the other) are called upon to protect fiercely and nurture the Osirian mummy (along with the child Horus) in various temples and ostensibly in the life-cycle of the Pharaoh. Within such cultic framework, the magical powers of Isis and Nephthys were seen as a primary, united force keeping chaos at bay. As part of this indispensable protective dyad, Nephthys was essential to the maintenance of ma'at, or "balance," for the good of temple, town, kingdom, and royal household.

As a chief mortuary goddess (along with Isis, Neith, and Serqet), Nephthys was one of the protectresses of the sacred Canopic jars and of the genii Hapi, in particular. Hapi (one of the Sons of Horus) guarded the embalmed lungs and, as his Mistress, Nephthys was a goddess capable of delivering the "breath of life" to the deceased via her wings. Thus, we find Nephthys endowed with the epithet, "Nephthys of the Bed of Life," (cf. tomb of Tuthmosis III, Dynasty XVIII) in direct reference to her regenerative priorities on the embalming table. In the city of Memphis, Nephthys was duly honored with the title "Queen of the Embalmer's Shop," and there associated with the _jackal_-headed god _Anubis_ as patron [9].

Nephthys' greatest role was clearly as the stalwart companion and reflection of her sister Isis. Because of the power shared between the two sisters, Egyptologist Claude Traunecker reminds us that ..".it is indeed not astonishing that the ancient Egyptians had recourse to Nephthys" [10]. In an abundance of temple texts and inscriptions, Nephthys quite often was described as a youthful, nubile, and exceedingly beautiful goddess—attributes which would facilitate her later identification with Hathor (or perhaps proceed from that identification). While intrinsically related to Isis in almost every aspect, Nephthys yet retained certain qualities that differentiated her from her sister: she was, seemingly deliberately, the more intangible, unpredictable half of the dyad.

At the same time, Nephthys was considered a festive deity whose rites (in various locales) could mandate the liberal consumption of beer. In various reliefs at Edfu, Dendera, and Behbeit, Nephthys is depicted receiving lavish beer-offerings from the Pharaoh, which she would "return", using her power as a beer-goddess "that [the pharaoh] may have joy with no hangover." Elsewhere at Edfu, for example, Nephthys is a goddess who gives the Pharaoh power to see "that which is hidden by moonlight." This fits well with more general textual themes that consider Nephthys to be a goddess whose unique domain was darkness, or the perilous edges of the desert.

Rarely, Nephthys could appear as one of the goddesses who assists at childbirth. One ancient Egyptian myth (preserved in the beloved <u>Papyrus Westcar</u>) recounts the story of Isis, Nephthys, Meskhenet, and Heqet as traveling dancers in disguise, assisting the wife of a priest of Amun-Re as she prepares to bring forth sons who are destined for fame and fortune. This "fairy godmother" role would not, however, prove to be a prominent motif in the general perception of Nephthys; she remained a deity far more associated with the final stages of life than with its beginnings.

Even so, Nephthys's healing skills and status as direct counterpart of Isis, steeped, as her sister in "words of power," are evidenced by the abundance of <u>faience</u> amulets carved in her likeness, and by her presence in a variety of magical papyri that sought to summon her famously altruistic qualities to the aid of mortals [11].

Cults of Nephthys

Contrary to the majority of commentators, Nephthys was not a neglected goddess in ancient Egypt who possessed no temple, nor worship of her own. As Chief Counterpart of Isis, member of the Great Ennead, and mighty guardian of Osiris and Horus, Nephthys was considered to be a rather formidable member of the wider pantheon. Within the realm of myth and temple cult, ancient Egyptian deities ultimately were defined by the company they kept and, in this case, Nephthys was undeniably a very major divinity. She was one of the few deities known and revered by all Egyptians, in virtually all territories. Relatively recent archaeological excavations corroborate ancient papyri and temple texts, shedding new light upon this heretofore underrated goddess.

For example, the Ramesside Pharaohs were particularly devoted to Set's prerogatives and, in the 19th <u>Dynasty</u> , a temple of Nephthys called the "House of Nephthys of Ramesses-Meriamun" was built or refurbished in the town of <u>Sepermeru</u>, midway between Oxyrhynchos and Herakleopolis, on the outskirts of the <u>Fayyum</u> and quite near to the modern site of Deshasheh. Here, as <u>Papyrus Wilbour</u> notes in its wealth of taxation records and land assessments, the temple of Nephthys was a specific foundation by Ramesses II, located in close proximity to (or within) the precinct of the enclosure of Set. To be certain, the House of Nephthys was one of fifty individual, land-owning temples delineated for this portion of the Middle Egyptian district in <u>Papyrus Wilbour</u>. The fields and other holdings belonging to Nephthys's temple were under the authority of two Nephthys-prophets (named Penpmer and Merybarse) and one (mentioned) <u>wa'ab</u> priest of the goddess.

While certainly affiliated with the "House of Set," the Nephthys temple at Sepermeru and its apportioned lands (several acres) clearly were under administration distinct from the Set institution [12]. The Nephthys temple was a unique establishment in its own right, an independent entity. According to

300

Papyrus Wilbour [13], another "House of Nephthys of Ramesses-Meriamun" seems to have existed to the north, in the town of Su, closer to the Fayyum region.

Interestingly, yet another (probably contemporaneous) temple of Nephthys seems to have existed in the town of Punodjem. The Papyrus Bologna records a complaint lodged by a prophet of the temple of Set in that town regarding undue taxation in his regard. After making an introductory appeal to "Re-Horakhte, Set, and Nephthys" for the ultimate resolution of this issue by the royal Vizier, the prophet (named Pra'emhab) laments his workload. He notes his obvious administration of the "House of Set" and adds: "I am also responsible for the ship, and I am responsible likewise for the House of Nephthys, along with a heap of other temples." [14].

While the House-of-Nephthys in (ostensibly) Punodjem is not explicitly said to be a foundation of Ramesses II, it may be that Ramesses II founded a series of "temples of Nephthys" (as consort of Set) in order to complement the larger establishments dedicated to her spouse, much in the same way that the smaller temple of Nefertari at Abu Simbel was complementary to (and a dependency of) the "Great Temple" at Abu Simbel. In the roster provided by Papyrus Wilbour, no other divine-consort boasted a land-owning temple of their own within any particular town dominated by a male god. Apparently, Nephthys was deemed quite important enough to merit her own independent sanctuaries.

In any event, as "Nephthys of Ramesses-Meriamun," the goddess and her shrine(s) were under the particular endorsement of Ramesses II. The foundations of the Set and Nephthys temples at Sepermeru finally were discovered and identified in the 1980s, and the Nephthys temple was no mere chapel—rather, it was a notable, self-sustaining temple complex within the Set enclosure [15].

Likewise, there can be little doubt that a cult of Nephthys existed in the temple and great town of Herakleopolis, north of Sepermeru. A near life-sized statue of Nephthys (currently housed in the Louvre) boasts a curiously altered inscription. The basalt image originally was stationed at Medinet-Habu, as part of the cultic celebration of the Pharaonic "Sed-Festival," but obviously was transferred at some point to Herakleopolis and the temple of Herishef therein. The cult-image's inscription originally pertained to "Nephthys, Foremost of the Sed [Festival] in the Booth of Annals" (at Medinet-Habu), but was re-inscribed or re-dedicated to "Nephthys, Foremost of the [Booths of] Herakleopolis."

This sort of opportunistic transfer of various cult images from one locale to another was not uncommon in ancient Egypt, and the installation of a cult statue of Nephthys at the temple of Harishef in Herakleopolis would have been fitting, since Nephthys already was a goddess with her own shrines in the immediate vicinity (i.e Sepermeru, Su, Punodjem). Moreover, a "prophet of Nephthys" is indeed attested for the town of Herakleopolis in the 30th Dynasty [16].

Chief Goddess of Nome VII

Nephthys also was, in Egyptian mythology and temple rites, oft-considered the unique protectress of the Sacred Phoenix, or the <u>Bennu</u> Bird. This role may have stemmed from a specialized and early association in her native Heliopolis, which was renowned for its "House of the Bennu" temple. In this role, Nephthys was given the name "Nephthys-Kheresket," and a wealth of temple texts from Edfu, Dendara, Philae, Kom Ombo, El Qa'la, Esna, and others corroborate the late identification of Nephthys as the supreme goddess of UE Nome VII, where another shrine existed in honor of the <u>Bennu</u>. Nephthys also was the goddess of the "Mansion of the <u>Sistrum</u>" in Hwt-Sekhem (Gr. Diospolis Parva), the chief city of Nome VII. There, Nephthys was the primary protectress of the resident Osirian relic, of the Bennu Bird, and of the local Horus/Osiris manifestation, the god Neferhotep. [6].

Indeed, a priest of "Nephthys of Hwt", <u>Diospolis Parva</u>, is mentioned in the <u>Book of the Dead</u> preserved at the <u>Louvre</u> in Paris. This Book of the Dead belonged to the mummy of a Theban-based priest named, Nes-Min. Another member of cult personnel, a male "Dancer of Nephthys", also is recorded for a Nome VII temple in Papyrus Moscou. Even more interesting, perhaps, we find that a female cult staff-member called the "hairdresser of

Nephthys" (i.e. of her sacred image in the temple naos) is noted in the 30th Dynasty [17]. This indicates that the overall cult of Nephthys must have been relatively elaborate in Diospolis Parva, particularly after the Late Period. As patron goddess of her own nome, this should not surprise the contemporary observer.

Though Nephthys was unquestionably the chief totemic goddess of Nome VII's district, city, and temple, she reigned there in a "first among equals" capacity connected with the usual Osirian college, and likewise through a close identification of her personality with that of Hathor, who reigned in nearby Dendera. In Hout-Sekhem and its nome, Nephthys (particularly in her guise as Khereset) appears to have served as preeminent "Mistress" of the various Osirian ceremonies, much in the way that Isis served in such singular capacity at Behbeit, in the Delta. Moreover, the presence of Nephthys is not at all attested in association with Diospolis Parva until the Late Period and Greco-Roman times, leading us to believe that her particular prominence (though indisputable) was something of an innovation. [18]. It is important to mention that the goddess Anukis appears to have served as a cultic "bridge" to the eminence of Nephthys in her later incarnation as main tutelary and "protective" goddess of the region.

Related to this last aspect, there is at least one surviving temple of Nephthys at Komir in Upper Egypt, between Esna and El Kab. In this town,

Nephthys was associated with the goddess <u>Anukis</u>. At Komir, Nephthys was honored especially for her role as the chief protectress of the standard Osirian relic residing at nearby <u>Esna</u>. The ruined sanctuary at Komir preserves two niches—one for Nephthys and one for Anukis, while the rear exterior wall of the temple preserves an elaborate "Hymn to Nephthys" from the Roman Emperor <u>Antoninus Pius</u>. In this hymn, the Emperor notes that Nephthys is the "Mistress of many festivals...who loves the day of festival, the goddess for whom men and women play the tambourine." There, too, Nephthys is called, "The very great Nephthys...Queen of human beings...Mistress of Drunkenness." She is identified closely with her alter-ego, <u>Seshat</u>, particularly as the entity who "establishes order for all the gods." This idea of Nephthys as the goddess who "organizes," or "makes whole" the entire divine <u>pantheon</u> is an ancient epithet stemming from the Pyramid Texts themselves. This epithet reinforces and elaborates upon the particularly unique (and enigmatic) role of Nephthys as a decidedly "Useful" cosmic force, one who apparently, acts for the organizational benefit of all deities. During the great Osirian festivals at Esna, associated with the temple of Khnum, it was specifically the cult-image of Nephthys that made the "journey" as official ambassador of Komir.

Most astonishing of all, the extant inscriptions of the Nephthys temple (and particularly her "hymn") at Komir make absolutely no mention of Isis whatsoever, despite references to a multitude of associated deities, including Osiris and Horus. This occurrence leads the observer to ponder the possibility that Nephthys was indeed a theologically specialized "alter ego" of Isis from the very beginning, or whether, in specific locales where the Two Sisters were not working in congress (as usual), the need to exalt Nephthys led to a determined effort to "oust" her greater sister from the scene entirely. As cited above (Traunecker), Nephthys was a goddess of much more clout than previously understood; in certain districts (Nome VII) she potentially could supersede her sister, though this was, by far, the exception rather than the proverbial "rule."

Nevertheless, the association of Nephthys with Anukis extends beyond Komir to the First Cataract region near Aswan and Philae, where the resident divine triad composed of Khnum, Satis, and Anukis was identified with (and superseded by) Osiris, Isis, and Nephthys around the Late Period.[19].

There was also a cult of Nephthys at Qaw El Kebir or Antaeopolis, where the goddess was worshipped in the rather large temple as the companion of the warrior deity Antiwey, a fusion of Horus and Set [20]. A "prophet of Nephthys" is attested for this town by the Chicago Stela and though the massive Greco-Roman sanctuary was washed away by a flood in the 19th century, a noteworthy painted relief of Nephthys and "Antaeus" can still be found etched into the cliffside quarries near the site.

At Mo'Alla, Nephthys was worshipped as the consort of another war-like god, Hemen. In contrast to her general perception as a childless divinity, Nephthys gave birth to Hemen's daughter in this cult locale. There exist other toponyms in various papyri and temple inscriptions that allude to possibly unique cult-towns of Nephthys (e.g. "Nephthys of Ihy," "Pr-Nephthys"), but such examples cannot at this time be considered verifications of cult.

It merits note, however, that Nephthys was one of the chief deities at Edfu, where she was the object of her own festival day called, "The Heart of Nephthys Rejoices" [1]. The national Festival of Nephthys was held on her birthday—the last of the five "epagomenal" days at the end of the Egyptian calendar. Nephthys, meanwhile, was a particularly dangerous goddess at Edfu, and, in her form of "Merkhetes," was associated with the lioness-goddesses Mehyt and Sekhmet. Nephthys' fiery breath is one of the forces that serves to protect the sanctuary of this great complex. There exists a chapel at Edfu dedicated to the triad of Mehyt, Nephthys, and Nekhbet. Nephthys also is associated at Edfu with the goddess Seshat, Mistress of the Temple Library and Keeper of Royal Annals. Based upon this evidence (and testimony dating from as early as the Pyramid Texts), we may entertain the likelihood that Seshat was indeed a derivative "form" of Nephthys (or vice-versa). Elsewhere, we discover from inscriptions at Behbeit that Queen Berenike considered herself the *"priestess of Isis and of Nephthys" (cf. Forgeau, above). Again, the union of the Two Sisters as powerful and almost inseparable complementary forces is underscored, both in the realm of myth and in the more crucial, daily domain of temple cult.*

Basically, Nephthys was everywhere. Even considering the late aspect of her prominence in places such as Hwt-Sekhem, she was a goddess who could, within the history of ancient Egyptian religion, merit New Kingdom temples and shrines of her own, and patronize her own district (Nome VII), which is all the more intriguing, given the clear superiority of her sister, Isis. The relationship between the Two Sisters is thus worthy of further, deeper inspection and study.

Unique instances of cult being noted, it must nevertheless be remembered that Nephthys was most widely and usually worshipped in ancient Egypt as part of a consortium of temple deities. Therefore, it should not surprise us that her cult images could likely be found as part of the divine entourage in temples at Kharga, Kellis, Deir el-Hagar, Koptos, Dendereh, Philae, Sebennytos, Busiris, Shenhur, El Qa'la, Letopolis, Heliopolis, Abydos, Thebes, Dakleh Oasis, and indeed throughout Egypt [21]. In most cases, Nephthys found her typical place as part of a triad alongside Osiris and Isis, or Isis and Horus, or Isis and Min, or as part of a quartet of deities. It is perhaps, in this way that Nephthys best fulfilled her role as an important national deity whose ideal

308

function was to provide powerful assistance to her associates in a great variety of temple cults—a truly "Useful" and "Excellent" goddess, as her primary epithets reflect.

1. ^ *a b* P. Wilson, 'A Ptolemaic Lexikon: A Lexicographical Study of the Texts in the Temple of Edfu', OLA 78, 1997

2. ^ Versuch über Nephthys, in: A. B. Lloyd [Hrsg.], Studies in Pharaonic Religion and Society in Honour of J. G. Griffiths, London 1992, 186-188

3. ^ Sauneron, Elephantine, Beitrage Bf. 6, 46 n.d.; Traunecker, Karnak VII, 184 n. 2; Cauville, 'Essai,' 152 n.7

4. ^ K.A. Kitchen, Ramesside Inscriptions, 1993, Blackwell

5. ^ B. Porter/R. Moss, Topographical Bibliography of Ancient Egyptian Hieroglyphic Texts, Reliefs, and Paintings. II. Theban Temples. Oxford Second Edition

6. ^ *a b* Sauneron, Beitrage Bf. 6, 46; C. Traunecker, Le temple d'El-Qal'a. Relevés des scènes et des textes. I' Sanctuaire central. Sanctuaire nord. Salle des offrandes 1 à 112

7. ^ James P. Allen, Peter Der Manuelian, 'The Pyramid Texts' SBL, 2005

8. ^ Levai, Jessica. "Nephthys and Seth: Anatomy of a Mythical Marriage", Paper presented at The 58th Annual Meeting of the American Research Center in Egypt, Wyndham Toledo Hotel, Toledo, Ohio, Apr 20, 2007.http://www.allacademic.com/meta/p176897_index.html

9. ^ J. Berlandini, p. 41-62, Varia Memphitica, VI - La stèle de Parâherounemyef, BIFAO 82

10. ^ El-Qa'la Temple, Traunecker, Ed. Quirke, 'The Temple in Ancient Egypt' Reeves C.N. 1996

11. ^ A. Gutbub, J. Bergman, Nephthys découverte dans un papyrus magique in Mélanges, Publications de la recherche, université de Montpellier, Montpellier, FRANCE, 1984

12. ^ 'Land Tenure in the Ramesside Period' by S. Katary, 1989

13. ^ Section 1. 28

14. ^ Papyrus Bologna 1094, 5, 8-7, 1

15. ^ 'Les Deesses de l'Egypte Pharaonique', R. LaChaud, 1992, Durocher-Champollion

16. ^ Forgeau, 'Pretres Isiaques,' BIFAO 84, 155-157

17. ^ Forgeau, BIFAO 84, 155-157; Vienna Stela

18. ^ P. Collombert, "Les stèles tardives de Hout-sekhem (Hout-sekhem et le septième nome de Haute-Égypte II)", RdE 48 (1997), pp. 15-70, pl. I-VII

19. ^ FM. Es-Saghir and D. Valbelle: Komir. I. The Discovery of Komir Temple. Preliminary Report. II. Deux hymnes aux divinités de Komir : Anoukis et Nephthys [avec 2 dépliants et 4 planches]BIFAO 84

20. ^ E. Graefe, Nephthys, Lexikon der A, 457-460, 1975

21. ^ BIFAO website

INDEX

Caelums- Heavens that exist inside the Chakras. The are seven main calums and thousand lesser calums. In India, Caelums are called Lokas. The seven main Caelums are:

SATURNUS CAELUM (ALM-e-VAKTYA) The First Awakening

After innumerable births of devotion to the path, the mystic enters Saturnus Caelum. The mystic loses consciousness of the earth realm and moves past the astral world. The deity that reflects the mystic's journey appears and reveals the persons individual path. There is no group conscious religion here, only the way that the person will become realized. Swirling circles of light take over the person as they experience the bliss of the deity present. This is the first spiritual enchantment (Samadhi in India). At this stage there is no more evolution, the mystic now enters the stage of involution- the process of unwinding all their impressions (samskaras) to merge into the deity that reflects their highest self.

JOVE CEALUM (ALM-e-RUHANI) The Realm of Enlightenment

Jove Caelum is the home to the Elysian Fields where there are faires, nymphs, satyrs and where the mind manifests the bliss of the hearts desire. When the mystic enters Jove Caelum, he/she becomes absorbed in the music of the sirens. The music is so enchanting that the mystic stays absorbed for days. There are 330 million angels on this realm. The Elysian Fields is the resting place for the souls of the heroes and virtuous men. The ancients often distinguished between two such realms-the islands of the blessed and the Lethean Fields of Pluto. The first of these, also known as the White Island was an afterlife realm reserved for the heroes and saints of myth. It was an island paradise located in the far western streams of the river Okeanos and ruled over by the Titan King-Kronos or Rhadamanthys, a son of Zeus. The second Elysium was a netherworld realm located in the depths of Hades beyond the river Lethe. Its fields were promised to the initiates of the mysteries who had lived a virtuous life. The Gods of the mysteries associated with the passage of the initiates to Elysium after death include Persephone, Lakkhos (the Eleusinian Hermes or Dionysus), Triptolemos, Hecate, Zagreus (the Orphic Dionysus), Melinoe (the Orphic Hecate) and Makaria. At this stage of the path, the mystic starts to develop mystical powers. All the energies of the Elysian Fields can be manifested in the material world if it is progressive to the individual's journey.

MAVORS CAELUM (ALM-e-KUDASI) Indra Loka-the Realm of Jove

Although all the power of Jove Caelum belongs to Jove himself, he sits in Mavors Caelum as King of the World beneath him. When the mystic enters Mavors Caelum, he gains more control over energy and he can now perform major miracles. The eyes of the mystic are swollen and often completely red from the intoxicating power of this realm. Whereas the mystic is intoxicated with the experience and power of angels on the Jove Caelum, here, on Mavors Caelum, he/she becomes intoxicated with his own energy.

VENUS CAELUM (ALM-e-MAHFAZ) The Realm of Universal Power

When the mystic travels to the fourth plane, he/she has infinite power and can create worlds merely by thought and destroy them as well. This is the home of the shape-shifter and there is no feat that this mystic cannot achieve. In ancinet Roman/Graeco myths, this was the abode of the High Witch. Aphrodite would give this mystic the power to enchant the whole universe. This realm was the most difficult because the person has to be in complete control of their thoughts. If the mystic abused this power, Aphrodite or a Master would turn them to stone and start the whole evolution of the person all over again.

MERCURIUS CAELUM (ALM-e-ISRAR) The Realm of Pure Knowledge

On Mercurius Caelum, the mystic trades in the world of power for divine knowledge. The voice of the Mother is spoken directly to the heart. Mercury (Greek-Hermes/Hindu-Buddha) opens the world of divine knowledge. Although the mystic lets go of power, he is in control of the thoughts of those on Venus Caelum. Here the mystic is completely safe and a friend of God. The music of Mercurius Caelum is so enchanting that the mystic will stay absorbed for months at a time. The music is the infinite OMNE (OM in Hinduism and Buddhism) and it continually pierces the heart's infinite intelligence.

LUNA CAELUM (PIR) The Realm of Longing

It is here the separation between man and God is so unbearable that the mystic weeps and the tears just flow from the experience of separation of lover and beloved. The Goddess Luna opens the door to the ocean of wine and love and the mystic is destroyed. Luna Caelum is the home of the Archangels and Luna is their Queen. On Luna Caelum, the person has no karma and their only desire is to unite with the beloved deity. When the person starts to unite with the beloved, Hecate in her highest form as the Black Sun (Nirvan), destroys the last imprint of the mystic.

SOL CAELUM (ARS-e-MAULA/NIVAKALPA SAMADHI)

Sol Caelum is the merging of the spirit into the ocean of light, the end of reincarnation

Chakras- (derived from the Sanskrit *cakraṃ*, is a Sanskrit word that
translates as "wheel" or "turning."
Chakra is a concept referring to wheel-like vortices which, according to

traditional Indian medicine, are believed to exist in the surface of the etheric double of man. The Chakras are said to be "force centers" or whorls of energy permeating, from a point on the physical body, the layers of the subtle bodies in an ever-increasing fan-shaped formation (the fans make the shape of a love heart). Rotating vortices of subtle matter, they are considered the focal points for the reception and transmission of energies. Seven major Chakras or energy centers (also understood as wheels of light) are generally believed to exist, located within the subtle body.

It is typical for Chakras to be depicted in either of two ways:

- Flower-like

- Wheel-like

In the former, a specific number of petals are shown around the perimeter of a circle. In the latter, a certain number of spokes divide the circle into segments that make the Chakra resemble a wheel or Chakra. Each Chakra possesses a specific number of segments or petals.

Much of the original information on Chakras comes from the Upanishads, which are difficult to date because they are believed to have been passed down orally for approximately a thousand years before being written down for the first time between 1200–BCE.

Hydra- In Greek mythology, the **Lernaean Hydra** (Greek: (*Λερναία Ὕδρα*) was an ancient nameless serpent-like chthonic water beast (as its name evinces) that possessed 7 or 9 heads— the poets mention more heads than the vase-painters could paint—and poisonous breath so virulent even her tracks were deadly. The Hydra of Lerna was killed by Heracles as one of his Twelve Labours. Its lair was the lake of Lerna in the Argolid, though archaeology has borne out the myth that the sacred site was older even than the Mycenaean city of Argos since Lerna was the site of the myth of the Danaids. Beneath the waters was an entrance to the Underworld, and the Hydra was its guardian.

Hydra II- In Jade Luna's philosophy, Hydra is a "corporeal energy" - an unconscious, instinctive or libidinal force or power, envisioned either as a goddess or else as a sleeping serpent coiled at the base of the spine, hence it is a 'serpent power' equated with Kundalini.

Hydra energy force can be "awakened" by Hecate.

In India awakening Hydra takes place by prepared by yogic austerities such as pranayama, or breath control, physical exercises, visualization, and chanting. It rises from muladhara Chakra up a subtle channel at the base of the spine (called *Sushumna*), and from there to top of the head merging with the sahasrara, or crown Chakra. The awakening is not a physical occurrence. It consists exclusively of development in consciousness. With awakening of the Hydra our consciousness expands and we become more aware of the truth When Hydra power is conceived as a goddess, then, when it rises to the head, it unites itself with the Being (TYPHON). Then mystic becomes engrossed in deep meditation and infinite bliss. The arousing of Hydra is said to be the one and only way of attaining Divine Wisdom. Self-Realization is said to be equivalent to Divine Wisdom or Gnosis or what amounts to the same thing: Self-Knowledge. The awakening of the Hydra shows itself as "awakening of inner knowledge" and brings with itself pure joy, pure knowledge and pure love.

However, like every form of energy one must also learn to understand spiritual energy. In order to be able to integrate this spiritual energy, careful purification and strengthening of the body and nervous system are required beforehand. By trying to force results, considerable psychic disturbances and at times even permanent mental damage can occur. A spiritual master who walked this path before is required to guide the mystic. Often will be found that negative experiences occurred only when acting without appropriate guidance or ignoring advice.

Kundalini can only be awakened through the grace of a Siddha-Guru who awakens the Kundalini shakti of his discipline through shaktipat, or blessing A Siddha Guru is a spiritual teacher, a master, whose identification with the Supreme Self is uninterrupted.

Nadis-(the Sanskrit for "tube, pipe") are the channels through which, in traditional Indian medicine and spiritual science, the energies of the subtle body are said to flow. They connect at special points of intensity called Chakras. Nadis seem to correspond to the meridians of traditional Chinese medicine

White Matter- is one of the two components of the central nervous system and consists mostly of myelinated axons. White matter tissue of the freshly cut brain appears pinkish white to the naked eye because myelin is composed largely of lipid tissue veined with capillaries. Its white color is due to its usual preservation in formaldehyde. A 20 year-old male has around 176,000 km of myelinated axons in his brain.

The other main component of the brain is Grey Matter (actually pinkish tan due to blood capillaries). A third colored component found in the brain that appears darker due to higher levels of melanin in dopaminergic neurons than its nearby areas is the substantia nigra.

Jade Sol Luna

Hecate devotee, Jade S. Luna is the first Westerner ever to reconstruct Jyotish (Hindu Astrology) into a Greco-Roman format. He became certified in Astrology from the A.F.A in Arizona, Dynah Academy in India and the A.I.V.S in Santa Fe New Mexico. Luna has written for several magazines including *Hinduism Today* and Luna has been featured on several Radio shows across the world.

Jade Luna has traveled extensively around the planet, lecturing and conducting workshops on Astrology and Ancient Roman-Greco mysticism. Jade has traveled to India more than 30 times and spent a great deal of time with various teachers, Saints and Sadhu's in Asia.

Jade Luna consults with people privately. He usually presents a few seminars each year at various locations world wide.

During and after Luna's formal Astrological training, Bhau Kalchuri (disciple of Meher Baba) and Kal Babaji (Khajuraho India), tutored him in advanced mysticism and other forms of classical Indian lore. Jade Luna has now transformed his Indian studies into a Greco-Roman practice, showing the spiritual connection that the Ancient Mediterranean had with India.

Jade Luna is the author of *Hecate: Death, Transition and Spiritual Mastery, Hecate II: The Awakening of Hydra* and will be releasing a series of Astrology books in the near future. Jade has been one of the most successful Astrologers in the world and has maintained a high level practice for over 16 years. For more information go to: www. Hiddenmoon.com

General References:

Thank you *Yukiko Ito* for the tremendous work you have done on Hecate. (Blake) Bibliography Aeschylus. The Suppliant Maidens. Trans. Seth G. Benardete. The Complete GreekTragedies: Volume I Aeschylus. 4th ed. Eds. David Grene and Richmond Lattimore. Chicago: The U of Chicago P, 1991. Ankarloo, Bengt, and Stuart Clark, eds. Introduction. Witchcraft and Magic in Europe: Ancient Greece and Rome. Philadelphia: U of Pennsylvania P, 1999. xi-xvi. Apollonios Rhodios. The Argonautika: The Story of Jason and the Quest for the Golden Fleece. Trans. Peter Green. Berkeley: U of California P, 1997. Aristophanes. Wealth. Trans. Stephen Halliwell. Birds and Other Plays. Oxford: Oxford UP, 1998. Baroja, Julio Caro. The World of the Witches. 1961. Trans. O. N. V. Glendinning. Chicago: The U of Chicago P, 1964. Bell, Robert E. Women of Classical Mythology. New York: Oxford UP, 1991. Blake, William. Hecate or The night of Enitharmon's Joy. [http://www.tate.org.uk/servlet/Awork?id=799]. Dec. 2000. Bonnefoy, Yves, comp. Greek and Egyptian Mythologies. Trans. Wendy Doniger. Chicago: The U of Chicago P, 1991. Burkert, Walter. Greek Religion. 1977. Trans. John Raffan. Cambridge, MA: Harvard UP, 1985. Euripides. Helen. Trans. Richmond Lattimore. The Complete Greek Tragedies: Volume III Euripides. Eds. David Grene and Richmond Lattimore. Chicago: The U of Chicago P, 1992. ----------. The Medea. Trans. Rex Warner. The Complete

Greek Tragedies: Volume III Euripides. Eds. David
Grene and Richmond Lattimore. Chicago: The U of
Chicago P, 1992. Ferguson, John. Among the Gods:
An Archaeological Exploration of ancient Greek
Religion. New York: Routledge, 1989. Flint, Valerie.
"The Demonisation of Magic and Sorcery in Late
Antiquity." Witchcraft and Magic in Europe: Ancient
Greece and Rome. Eds. Bengt Ankarloo and Stuart
Clark. Philadelphia: U. of Pennsylvania P, 1999.
Gager, John G., ed. Curse Tablets and Binding Spells
from the Ancient World. New York: Oxford UP,
1992. Gimbutas, Marija. The Goddesses and Gods of
Old Europe, 6500-3500BC: Myths and Cult Images.
London: Thames and Hudson, 1982. ------------. The
Language of the Goddess. San Francisco: Harper
Collins, 1989. ------------. The Living Goddesses. Ed.
Miriam Robbins Dexter. Berkeley: U of California P,
1999. Gordon, Richard. "Imagining Greek and
Roman Magic." Witchcraft and Magic in Europe:
Ancient Greece and Rome. Eds. Bengt Ankarloo and
Stuart Clark. Philadelphia: U. of Pennsylvania P,
1999. Guthrie, W. K. C. Orpheus and Greek Religion.
Princeton: Princeton UP, 1993. Harris, Stephen L.,
and Gloria Platzner. Classical Mythology: Images and
Insights. 2nd. Ed. Mountain View, CA: Mayfield,
1998.   Hecate   Triformus.
[http://jblstatue.com/pages/hecate_triformu.html].
Dec. 2000. Hesiod. Theogony. Trans. Richmond
Lattimore. The Works and Days, Theogony, The
Shield of Herakles. 1959. Ann Arbor: The U of
Michigan P, 1965. Homeric Hymn to Demeter. Trans.

Apostolos N. Athanassakis. The Homeric Hymns. Baltimore: The Johns Hopkins UP, 1976. Johnston, Sarah Iles. Hecate Soteira: A Study of Hecate's Roles in the Chaldean Oracles and Related Literature. Atlanta: Scholars P, 1990. Kerenyi, Karl. Myth and Man: The Gods of the Greeks. Ed. Joseph Campbell. Trans. Norman Cameron. New York: Thames and Hudson, 1951. Luck, Georg. "Witches and Sorcerers in Classical Literature." Witchcraft and Magic in Europe: Ancient Greece and Rome. Eds. Bengt Ankarloo and Stuart Clark. Philadelphia: U. of Pennsylvania P, 1999. Nilsson, Martin P. Greek Folk Religion. 1940. Philadelphia: U of Pennsylvania, 1972. Ogden, Daniel. "Binding Spells: Curse Tablets and Voodoo Dolls in the Greek and Roman Worlds." Witchcraft and Magic in Europe: Ancient Greece and Rome. Eds. Bengt Ankarloo and Stuart Clark. Philadelphia: U. of Pennsylvania P, 1999. Ovid. Metamorphoses. 1955. Trans. Rolfe Humphries. Bloomington: Indiana UP, 1983. Pausanias. Guide to Greece Volume 1: Central Greece. 1971. Trans. Peter Levi. London: Penguin Books, 1979. -----------. Guide to Greece Volume 2: Southern Greece. 1971. Trans. Peter Levi. London: Penguin Books, 1979. -----------. Mythology and Monuments of Ancient Athens. Trans. Margaret de G. Verrall. New York: MacMillan and Co., 1890. Rice, David G., and John E. Stambaugh. Sources for the Study of Greek Religion. Missoula, MT: Scholars P, 1979. Roberts, Louis. Class lecture. Classics 402. State University of New York at Albany. 26 Sep. 2000. Theophrastus. The

Character Sketches. Trans. Warren Anderson. Iowa City: The Kent State UP, 1970. Von Rudloff, Robert. "The Horned Owl Library: Hecate in Early Greek Religion."
[http://www.islandnet.com/~hornowl/library/Hecate.html]. Nov. 2000.
Campbell, Joseph. (1990). Transformations of Myth Through Time. New
York: Harper & Row.Eliade, Mircea. (1969). Yoga: Immortality and Freedom, tr. Willard R.
Trask. Bollingen Series LVI. Princeton: Princeton University Press.

Mead, G. R. S. (1967). The Doctrine of the Subtle Body in Western
Tradition. Theosophical Publishing House.

Murphy, Michael. (1992). The Future of the Body: Explorations Into
the Further Evolution of Human Nature. New York: Jeremy
Tarcher/Putnam.

Onians, Richard Broxton. (1951). The Origins of European Thought About
the Body, the Mind, the Soul, the World, Time, and Fate. Cambridge:
Cambridge University Press.

Poortman, J. J. (1978). Vehicles of Consciousness: The Concept of

Hylic Pluralism. Vols. 1-4. Theosophical Publishing House.
Chakra images by Mara Berendt Friedman

Personal References

(1) *"The Mysteries of the Maiden and the Mother" by Glenn Turner*

(2) *Thank you John Osopaus for your excellent work on the subject*

(3) *"Inspired by Meher Baba"*

(4) *Sections on Kundalini and Chakras inspired by Swami Sivananda and David Frawley*

Artwork in this book by Maria Magdalene

The central part of this book is based upon the merging of Swami Sivavnda, Homerica, Ramakrishna, Meher Baba, Plato, OVID and Seneca. For, without them, this book would not exist. I bow to these masters for their incredible devotion to the truth.

Special thanks West: My Love Gianna, Devona at Ritual Promotions, Sheryl Lee, Lisa Sawoya, Janet Montgomery, Charles G. Leland, Lew Wirt and Pagan Radio Network, OVID

Special thanks East: Meher Baba, Bhau Kalchuri, Sivananda, Ramakrishna and Upasni Maharaj for their words are alive and well in this book. Tara Press INC,

JADE SOL LUNA BOOKS AND CD'S

Book-"Hecate I: Death, Transition and Spiritual Mastery"

"One of the most raw and intelligent visions on the Dark Mother or any form of Western spirituality to date!"~ Jyoti Chandranada-Hinduism Today

CD-Queen of the Crossroads

35 minutes of a spiritual journey into Hecate Luna. Possibly one of the most haunting chants to the Goddess Hecate. "Jana's hymn has great inner power and opened a powerful door of transformation!"-Whole Life Times

CD-Hecate Phantasmagoria

A masterful mix of Ancient Latin and Demotic Chanting with Greek instruments and powerful yet haunting ambient landscapes. This is a masterful meditative CD that plans to take the listener back to the Hellenistic era.

CD-Scorpio Invocatio

The Third CD release from the team of Jade Luna and Jordan James on CreateS. Records. This is a strong meditative chant that takes the listener deep into the constellation Scorpio, the home of the Greek Goddess Hecate. Deep droning undertones create a soundscape of intensity and transformation. Not your typical meditative CD, but something very real and original. A must for those that want to explore the deep subconscious.

CD-Zodiac Hymns

Another Jade Luna and Jordan James collection of Ambient chanting Cd's on CreateS Records. This CD is Pre-Augustas Latin Chanting to the Planetary Gods. It is an Ambient CD mixed with Egyptian and Greek undertones. Awesome for meditations that take you back to Ancient Rome and Greece.

CD-Silver Moon, Black Sun

This CD is a collection of the most powerful Latin, Greek and Demotic Hymns known. The tracks on these CD's can be used for overcoming fear, house clearings, the removing of negative energies, empowering stones, gaining inner strength, and most important... to invoke the power of the Feminine Divine! Out now on Legatus Records.

CD-Prakriti Vidya

Released in India in 2005, now available in the US. Jade Luna, noted for his gift in invocation, brings you the energy (shakti) of the nine main Hindu planets and the Goddess Dhumavati. A deep, droning meditation CD that brings the subconscious into consciousness. "A sanskrit masterpiece!" -Krisnananda Das

CD-Aghori Kali-The Ambient Journey of a Skull Girl

Jade Sol Luna in an ambient journey through the goddess Kali. Deep haunting yet melodic landscapes mixed with powerful sanskrit chanting. A must for those that want to meditate with the Aghori's. "An ambient Journey into the madness of Kali."-Hinduism Today

INDIA RESEARCH PRESS / TARA PRESS INTERNATIONAL

INDIA
Corporate Office -
B-4/22,Khajuraho - 110 029, INDIA
Telephone :   91-11-2369 4610 Telefax :   91-11-2471 8637

Editorial Office -

Flat #6, TRUST OFFICE - 110003, India.
Tel: 00.91.11.2469 4610, 2469 4855
TeleFAX: 00.91.11.24618637, 417 57 113

AMERICA

JSL INC Press.
14431 Ventura Blvd suite 538
Sherman Oaks CA 91423
www.hiddenmoon.com

copyright@jslinc.org Tarainternational/jslpress

www.ingramcontent.com/pod-product-compliance
Lightning Source LLC
Chambersburg PA
CBHW031041110426
42740CB00046B/248